Eugenics, Race and Intelligence in Education

Also available from Continuum

A Tribute to Caroline Benn, Melissa Benn and Clyde Chitty
Analysing Underachievement in Schools, Emma Smith
Education and Community, Dianne Gereluk
Schools and Religions, Julian Stern
Is Religious Education Possible?, Michael Hand

Eugenics, Race and Intelligence in Education

Clyde Chitty

With a foreword
by Tony Benn

continuum

Continuum International Publishing Group
The Tower Building
11 York Road
London
SE1 7NX

80 Maiden Lane, Suite 704
New York
NY
10038

www.continuumbooks.com

British Library Cataloguing-in-Publication Data
A catalogue record for this book is available from the British Library.

ISBN: 0-8264-8980-X (hardcover)

Library of Congress Cataloging-in-Publication Data
Chitty, Clyde.
  Eugenics, race, and intelligence in education / Clyde Chitty.
    p. cm.
  ISBN-13: 978-0-8264-8980-7 (hardcover)
  ISBN-10: 0-8264-8980-X (hardcover)
 1. Eugenics—Great Britain—History. 2. Eugenics—United States—History.
3. Intelligence tests—Great Britain—History. 4. Intelligence tests—United States—History. 5. Classism—Great Britain—History. 6. Racism—United States—History.
7. Education—Great Britain. 8. Nature and nurture. I. Title.

  HQ755.5.G7C55 2007
  363.9'20941—dc22

                                        2007017765

Typeset by Free Range Book Design & Production Ltd
Printed and bound in Great Britain by Biddles Ltd., King's Lynn, Norfolk

For my partner Chi in gratitude
for all his love and encouragement

Contents

Acknowledgements

My thanks are due to all my students at Goldsmiths College, past and present, who have never been reluctant to challenge many of the views expressed in this book and to provide alternative perspectives of their own. I must also acknowledge the debt I owe to Professor Roy Lowe who first made me aware of the relationship between eugenics, intelligence testing and the concept of racial purity when we were colleagues at the University of Birmingham in the early 1990s. Above all, I owe a special debt of gratitude to Margaret Brittain, who has played such a major role in the preparation of this manuscript in its final form. In addition, she has suggested a number of the books and articles that I have used in support of my arguments. Of course, the errors that remain are very much my own.

Clyde Chitty
January 2007

Foreword

This is a very important book, scholarly, readable and relevant, by a distinguished educationalist whose commitment to teaching and to his pupils over many years has uniquely equipped him to explore the influence of eugenics on the ongoing debate about the future of our schools which concerns everyone in society.

We are regularly told that the object of our educational system must be to improve overall standards and provide the highest possible level of achievement, an argument that is actually calculated to win wide support for a system of selection and encourage us to distrust comprehensive schools which are designed to break down segregation as the best way forward, on the grounds that they represent a form of social engineering.

Professor Chitty, in this formidable historical review of educational policy, has revealed the thinking which lies behind these arguments and offers us, instead, an explanation which reveals that the concepts of inherent ability which are used to justify selection are themselves an unscientific form of social engineering which preserve the privileges of a certain race, sex or social class.

These privileges originated with the claim of those who acquired power by inheritance – the Monarchy and the Lords who owned the land, by conquest – that they were justified in elevating the victorious races over those whom they had conquered, and of men who were able to impose their power over women as the 'weaker sex'.

Given that knowledge is power and liberates those who have it or can acquire it, it is not hard to see why those in power do not want to share that power, and history is full of attempts to restrict access to knowledge for that very reason – from the Heresy Act of 1401, which made it an offence punishable by death for the laity to read the Bible, to the modern attempts to conceal government policies in the interest of security.

Access to education was always restricted to the rich, who could buy it, until technological advance made it necessary for others to be trained to be able to use it and out of that came the first developments in state education, but even today there are those who are clearly suspicious that if it were available to all on the same basis their control might be eroded.

Hence the tripartite system introduced after the passing of the 1944 Education Act which identified three sorts of mind, the academic, the technical and the rest, a distinction that was breached only by allowing some of the 'cleverest' working-class pupils to attend grammar schools which gave a sort of legitimacy to them.

But behind all this thinking lie the ideas of those who believe in eugenics, and this is the theme of the book linking the subject with those who have argued that selection is the way of the world and that those in power have a duty to preserve the purity of the elite in order to preserve society.

In their crudest and most dangerous form, these were the ideas that lay at the heart of fascism where Hitler could openly speak of the Germans as the 'master race' and feel justified in persecuting Jews and in pursuing policies to deal with the feeble-minded, both designed to preserve Nazi power.

Without drawing any simplistic political parallels, the same ideas can be identified as influencing those social practitioners today who speak on the one hand about 'giftedness' and at the same time warn that dangerous characteristics can be identified early in life and must be addressed as if they were inherent, instead of being the result of conditions in society that need a political response.

Here is where Professor Chitty's analysis will make most sense to those who have concluded that the arguments of many who claim to want to raise standards are actually used against the extension of a rounded education to the population as a whole, and that some of the most vociferous voices making this point see selection as a way of restricting education and standards for their own reasons.

And here is where the League Tables can be seen to play a key role, for if educational failure can be identified and denounced, those who have failed can be presented as people upon whom education would be wasted and for the rest of their lives they will be branded in that way, an absurdity that has been proved time and again by the advantages that Adult Education provides.

To control a nation, it is necessary to frighten, divide and demoralize it and the present educational system has many features for those who want to do just that: fear of failure; the division between schools and the demoralization of those who have fallen behind.

Apart from the brilliance of this book, its author deserves a hearing because he has consistently encouraged, united and respected his own pupils and his 2001 inaugural lecture at Goldsmiths College, which I attended, was about eugenics and made a tremendous impact on the audience just because it was being delivered by a teacher who had lived out his life as an advocate and practitioner of the very ideas which stand in contrast with those he analyses and criticizes in this powerful and important book.

Tony Benn
23 April 2007

The Structure of the Book

The whole idea that intellectual ability or 'intelligence' is fixed and innate – and, moreover, that it is to be found almost exclusively among the offspring of the middle and upper classes – must be viewed against the background of centuries of opposition to the concept of mass state education. Chapter 1 describes the way in which fear at the prospect of an educated working class has formed such an important part of educational discourse in Britain since the invention of printing in the second half of the fifteenth century. Throughout the so-called modern era, there has been a strong view within the 'political establishment' that a policy of universal high-quality education would lead almost inevitably to widespread disaffection and popular revolt. In the period of religious upheaval following the Breach with Rome in the 1530s, there was much anxiety as to the use that could be made of the translated Bible as a handbook for the radical transformation of society. Even today, one of the ideas underpinning the debate about the relative merits of 'academic' and 'vocational' education is that we need to *educate* the middle class but merely to *train* the working class – a view which means that academic and vocational courses will never acquire equal status in Britain.

Chapter 2 focuses on the life and work of Francis Galton, explorer, scientist and statistician and second cousin of *On the Origin of Species* author Charles Darwin. It was actually Francis Galton who coined the term 'eugenics' – now commonly defined as the study of methods of *maintaining* and *improving* the innate quality of the human race, especially by selective breeding – and this was in his book *Inquiries into Human Faculty*, first published in 1883. Throughout his life, Galton sought to apply Darwinian principles to his analysis of human society; and, if natural selection had determined the fact that some human beings were clearly 'superior' to others, it was important to establish psychology as a *biological* science. In his studies of individual families, Galton set out to prove that 'genius' was inborn and confined almost exclusively to certain types of privileged beings with social standing and innate qualities of leadership.

Galton's eugenic theories soon acquired extraordinary popularity with novelists, poets and social reformers; and this is the subject of Chapter 3. In England, the Eugenics Education Society was founded in 1907, with the stated aim of 'furthering eugenic teaching and understanding in the home, in the schools and elsewhere'. This Society (known simply as the Eugenics Society after 1926) enjoyed a degree of influence out of all proportion to the actual size of its membership which was never particularly large. T. S. Eliot, Aldous and Julian Huxley, George Bernard Shaw, H. G. Wells and W. B. Yeats were all enthusiastic supporters of the Society's broad mission, as was birth control pioneer Marie Stopes. For many eugenicists – and this was particularly true of Aldous Huxley, Marie Stopes and H. G. Wells – of greatest concern was the alarming rate of population growth since the beginning of the nineteenth century, especially since this was most marked among members of the immigrant and working classes. In his 1905 novel *Kipps*, H. G. Wells described 'the extravagant swarm of new births' as 'the essential disaster of the nineteenth century'. Once Marie Stopes had acquired a national reputation for her persistent advocacy of family planning, it seemed to be the less populous well-to-do, rather than the despised lower orders, who were actually practising birth control; and in a situation already aggravated by the effects of the First World War, there were fears that the entire social fabric was in danger of being torn apart by an overpopulated proletariat. This was also a period when many intellectuals and policy-makers were exercised by fears of a deterioration in the nation's physical health, and in seeking to promote a model of 'national efficiency', they welcomed sterilization as a medical remedy to the problems of mental illness and the alleged fecundity of the mentally sick.

One of Francis Galton's most ardent disciples in England was Cyril Burt, who did more than anyone to advocate the widespread use of IQ (intelligence quotient) tests for the purpose of determining a child's 'innate' intelligence at the age of eleven; and this is the theme of Chapter 4. Burt's early work as a child psychologist was, in fact, largely concerned with the problem of mental deficiency – often referred to at the time as 'feeblemindedness' – and he wrote about this in *The Eugenics Review*, the Eugenics Society's very own journal launched in 1908. Believing that there was no such thing as 'acquired' feeblemindedness, Burt moved on to argue that all intelligence, or 'all-round intellectual ability', was inherited or innate, capable of being measured with accuracy and ease. As official educational psychologist to the LCC (London County Council) for nearly twenty years, from 1913 to 1932, Burt wielded enormous power and influence, and his unequivocal views on intelligence underpinned the recommendations of both the 1931 Hadow Report on *The Primary School* and the 1938 Spens Report on *Secondary Education*. It was these views that determined the precise nature of the structuring of the secondary education system after the passing of the 1944 Education Act.

Chapter 5 describes how, in the course of the 1950s, the validity of the eleven-plus selection procedure increasingly came under scrutiny, with many teachers and educationists beginning to have grave misgivings about Burt's confident assertions about innate intelligence. A number of children who had 'failed' the eleven-plus examination went on to acquire a respectable batch of GCE Ordinary Level passes at the age of sixteen and even gain entry to university, all of which seemed to prove that if such a thing as innate intelligence actually existed, it could hardly be measured with accuracy and ease or be satisfactorily distinguished from ability that had been acquired. A report of a special working party set up by the British Psychological Society, which was published in 1957, conceded that, since it was now obvious that many school pupils could actually *enhance* their IQ scores, it must be true that 'environmental' factors, however defined, had *some* effect on the development of abilities – and particularly in the early and teenage years. This rejection of Burt's doctrinaire approach, even if couched in somewhat cautious and moderate language, was one of the important factors which lay behind the growing support for the comprehensive ideal at the secondary level of schooling.

Somewhat paradoxically, just at the time when Cyril Burt's views were being effectively challenged in England, the debate about ability and intelligence in the United States was broadened to embrace issues of 'race' as well as of class; and this is the subject of Chapter 6. In 1969, Arthur Jensen published a very long article in *The Harvard Educational Review* with the title 'How Much can we Boost IQ and Scholastic Achievement?', which argued that just as working-class white children were inferior (in terms of their measured intelligence) to middle-class and upper-class white children, so black children were innately inferior to white children. Any attempt, however well-intentioned, to reverse this 'natural' state of affairs by means of compensatory educational programmes was obviously a tragic waste of time and money. It was, of course, inevitable that Jensen's main conclusions should be widely reported; and they were treated as if they were *scientific* findings, rather than hypotheses which he was advancing for examination and discussion, as he himself insisted. Their practical and political significance immediately became clear when they were quoted by lawyers in the Deep South of the United States in the campaign against integration in the schools. It was now argued that there should be all-black 'remedial' schools for 'backward' black pupils, with black children admitted to white schools only if they passed a number of demanding standardized tests.

Chapter 7 surveys our continuing preoccupation with eugenic ideas, particularly where concepts of intelligence are concerned.

Publication in America in 1994 of *The Bell Curve* by the late Richard J. Herrnstein and Charles Murray ensured that the debate about race and intelligence lost none of its ferocity, for this book was a skilful and well-publicized reiteration of the theories of Cyril Burt and Arthur Jensen. Herrnstein and Murray were also very critical of rival views of intelligence and, in particular, of the theory of 'multiple intelligences' advocated by Harvard psychologist Howard Gardner in his 1983 book *Frames of Mind*.

In England, official support by the New Labour Government for the setting of all pupils by ability in both primary and secondary schools has meant the pinning of ability labels on children from an early age.

At the same time, it needs to be stressed that there are groups of classroom teachers working in a number of countries, including England, who have *rejected* eugenic notions of fixed ability and are determined to base their teaching on an unshakeable belief in everybody's capacity to learn. The Conclusion argues that the key to human development is not *heredity* but *education*; and this was, in fact, one of the guiding principles of a 2004 book *Learning Without Limits*, compiled by a team of researchers at the University of Cambridge School of Education and based on the documented experiences of a group of nine classroom teachers who had freed themselves from determinist beliefs about ability and intelligence. A way forward that is truly liberating would seem to lie in classroom practice based upon a complex and multifaceted understanding of teaching and learning processes and of all the influences, both internal and external to the schools, that impinge on learning and achievement.

Introduction: Nature versus Nurture

For over a hundred years, psychologists and human biologists have been engaged in an often heated and acrimonious debate as to whether 'heredity' or the more vague and generalized category of 'environment' (encompassing a wide range of 'active' and 'passive' influences) should be viewed as *the* determining factor in the creation of human personality. For teachers and educationists, the debate has tended to focus on issues relating to the functioning of the human mind and the development of intellectual powers. The controversy is often expressed simply in terms of 'nature *versus* nurture', with some scientists choosing to adopt a 'middle of the road' position by declaring that *all* human beings are a product of a transaction between the two.

It seemed possible that the whole issue had been resolved when a front-page story appeared in the *Observer* on 11 February 2001 reporting the findings of two major groups of international scientists which had completed their initial analysis of the first human genetic map, known as 'the genome'. Under the banner headline 'Revealed: the secret of human behaviour', with the subheading: 'Environment, not genes, key to our life', the *Observer*'s Science Editor Robin McKie reported that the human genome possessed not between 100,000 and 150,000 genes as originally anticipated, but just 30,000. The source of Robin McKie's story was Dr Craig Venter, the American scientist whose private company Celera was in competition with an international consortium funded by taxes and charities. Details of the findings of the two groups had been circulated to journalists under embargo, but Dr Venter had broken the story at an open meeting held in Lyons on 9 February and Robin McKie had been one of those in the audience. Interviewed by McKie, Dr Venter argued that 'we simply do not have enough genes for the idea of biological determinism to be right. The wonderful diversity of the human species is not hard-wired in our genetic code. Our environments are critical'. Dr Venter went on to dismiss the idea, currently fashionable among a number of biologists and geneticists, that there were individual genes shaping human development and behaviour patterns, ranging from intellectual ability to sexual orientation and criminality, and even including political preference. Environment and human experience were *the* key factors in shaping the way human beings behaved; in other words, in Dr Venter's view, 'human beings were *not* the prisoners of their genes'.

Robin McKie's front-page story in the *Observer* was taken up by other newspapers in both Britain and America. 'Genome discovery shocks scientists: genetic blueprint contains far fewer genes than originally thought – DNA's importance downplayed' ran the headline to the story which appeared in the *San Francisco Chronicle*, also on Sunday 11 February 2001. The following day the *New York Times* had a story headlined: 'Analysis of human genome discovers far fewer genes than anticipated'.

Yet the *Observer* story did not, in fact, settle the debate about the origins of human behaviour. Many argued that knowledge of the *precise* number of genes in our make-up did nothing to enhance our understanding of human personality – and that, in any case, 30,000 was a large enough number to make every human being in the world unique, with characteristics that were primarily innate.

It might, of course, seem to many that all this enquiry and speculation is somewhat futile and depressing – of concern mainly to moral philosophers and to those who want to argue endlessly about issues of free will and determinism. Yet it can also be argued that at least in the area related to the development of abilities, the debate about nature *versus* nurture, with *nature* invariably triumphant, has had dire consequences for the education of millions of young people. And we surely need to ask why this debate has been pursued with such vigour in Britain and America.

This book is essentially a study of the way in which a belief in genetic determinism in the area of human intellectual capacity grew out of a set of ideas about sustaining and improving the quality of the human race – broadly covered by the term 'eugenics' and particularly influential in the first half of the twentieth century – and then went on to profoundly influence the structure of the British education system. While not wishing to argue that all those who still believe in the efficacy of intelligence testing or in the notion of fixed innate ability are either eugenicists or racists, this book does seek to demonstrate that the mental measurement movement has its origins in atavistic concerns about mental degeneracy and racial purity. It is further argued that a lingering belief in genetic determinism in the area of human ability has meant a failure to take on board the liberating concept of human educability.

Chapter 1

The 'Threat' of Mass Education

Introduction

As I have argued elsewhere (Chitty, 1992), England was the last
major country in Europe to create a national education system; and
even after the legislation creating such a system was passed in the
final decades of the nineteenth century, little pride was shown in the
reformers' achievement. The idea of abandoning the concept of
voluntaryism[1] and opting instead for making education a direct
concern of the state had all sorts of frightening implications for
many of the politicians of the 1870s and 1880s and seemed to fly
in the face of England's laissez-faire individualism where education
was concerned. There had, it is true, been an early attempt to
organize schools and colleges into a coordinated system of education
at the time of the sixteenth-century Reformation (see Simon, 1966)
and there had been a brief period of educational reform and
expansion after the execution of Charles I in 1649, but with the
Restoration of Charles II in 1660 came a virtual abandonment of
the interventionist role of the state in education provision.

Professor Andy Green has argued that what most distinguishes
English educational history in the 200-year period from 1660 to
1870 is 'the almost total absence of those state initiatives which
were so significant in continental development' (Green, 1990, p.
241). In Prussia, for example, Frederick II's compulsory attendance
laws in 1763 marked the first important move in the direction of
national education; and a national public system comprising
elementary and secondary schools was essentially in place by the
end of the 1830s. During Altenstein's period as Minister of
Education (1817–38), elementary education was extended and
regulated, thereby developing a high degree of mechanical
efficiency under centralized control.

In France, the central administrative apparatus for education was
created by Napoleon with the laws founding the *Université* (the

Napoleonic term for the whole system of schools and higher institutions) passed in 1806 and 1808. The Napoleonic *lycée* was
created as early as 1802 giving the state a strategic control over
secondary education; and it is possible to talk in terms of a full
judicial and administrative framework for national education by the
time of the Second Empire, which began life in 1852. It is also interesting to note that respect for the Revolutionary and Napoleonic
concept of education as a public function of the state has remained
a significant factor in French educational thought. This sense of
pride in past achievements certainly comes through in a key passage
in the Introduction to a bill of 1957 designed to reform the organization of schools:

> It was the Revolution which proclaimed officially, for the first
> time in France, 'the right to education as an essential right of all
> individuals' together with the Nation's duty 'to instruct all its
> citizens'. These principles were totally new in the school situation
> of that period. (quoted in Fraser, 1963, p. 5)

In England, on the other hand, it was only in 1870 that the Forster
Education Act – responding to the needs of a radically changing
society – laid the first foundations of a *national* system of education
by the introduction of state-*provided* and state-*maintained*
elementary schools under the control of around 2500 newly created
School Boards. And even this important piece of legislation –
designed to *fill the gaps* in existing church provision – did not
introduce compulsory education, just as it did not make state
education free. It was not until 1880 that school attendance
throughout the country was finally made compulsory, at least until
the age of ten, to be raised to eleven in 1893 and (except for children
employed in agriculture) to twelve in 1899. And it was not until
1891 that an Act was passed to make most elementary education
free.

The Reasons for England's Backwardness

England's reluctance to embrace the concept of state education has
been the subject of much debate among historians, though there is
agreement that it has its origins in the specific nature of the nation's
class structure and in the fears and prejudices of each of the major
groups making up society.

One theory popular among historians is that, despite the economic and social changes brought about by the Industrial Revolution, nineteenth century England failed to become a truly *middle-class* state and therefore lacked the incentive to develop a state system of education to meet *middle-class* needs. In his influential book *English Culture and the Decline of the Industrial Spirit, 1850–1980*, published in 1981, Martin J. Wiener argued that Britain's economic weakness for much of the twentieth century was due to an anti-industrial culture which had its roots in nineteenth-century aristo-cratic rule. The aristocratic oligarchy in Victorian England was possibly unique in its absorption of upwardly mobile middle-class families; and such absorption meant that the rising new business class of the nineteenth century found a firm pattern of life already mapped out for them (see Hobsbawm, 1968, pp. 63–5). Despite offering a curriculum that paid little or no attention to the scientific and the technical, the Victorian public schools enjoyed enormous popularity and prestige with industrialists, entrepreneurs and technological innovators. Even Isambard Kingdom Brunel (1806–59), arguably the greatest engineer of his generation, sent two sons to Harrow School, where they were hardly likely to be encouraged to follow their father's profession (see Bamford, 1967, p. 105). As Wiener has observed, 'the public schools' disparagement of specialized and practical studies reinforced the traditional content of the professional ideal – the imitation of the leisured landed gentleman – at the expense of the modern role of the professional as expert' (Wiener, 1981, p. 19). And this remarkable dominance of aristocratic amateur values meant a complete absence of that 'credentialist' or 'meritocratic' ethos which was such a marked influence on continental state education. For as long as the public schools retained their dominant role in public life and were able to absorb the sons of wealthy businessmen and industrialists, there was little incentive for the new bourgeoisie to create state schools with different values. Even when it was no longer possible for all the sons of the new middle class to gain admission to a public school, their parents invariably sought a grammar school as close as possible to the public school model.

Andy Green has argued (1990) that any convincing explanation for England's 'backwardness' in creating a fully fledged state education system would have to take account of the deep infusion of liberal individualism in both the landed and middle classes. In his view, what separated England from the major continental states was not only the predominance of landed, anti-capitalist culture, but the power of the individualist creed, which meant that all sections of the ruling class shared a marked hostility to the state and were deeply suspicious of the idea of state control of education. For the major part of the nineteenth century, political economy recognized only the individual. The public good was no more than the happiness of the greatest number of individuals, and this could be achieved only through the individual pursuit of enlightened self-interest. Only gradually did a section of the governing class adapt to the social and economic changes of the Victorian period and come to accept the idea that the greatest freedom for every individual was possible only within the framework of the collective state.

There remains a third reason why for so long the political elite in England felt that education provision should *not* be a concern of central government. Indeed, the very idea that the masses should be educated at all beyond a strictly primitive level was something to be viewed with alarm and trepidation. It is the story of this fear of mass education – dating back at least to the invention of printing in the second half of the fifteenth century and the translation of the New Testament into English in the 1520s and 1530s – that forms the substance of this chapter.

The Fear of Mass Education

In the sixteenth and seventeenth centuries, teaching the masses to read was seen as a foolhardy and potentially dangerous enterprise, particularly if it gave the common people access to God's Word in English. Historian Linda Colley has summed up the situation in a succinct paragraph:

> In the beginning was the Word. But, apart from the very educated and the very rich, few were able to read it. Then came the invention of the printing press and the Protestant Reformation. And the Bible began to speak with many tongues. (Colley, 1993, p. 31)

It was certainly clear to the political elite of the Reformation period that the translated Bible could be very useful as a handbook for all manner of radical and indeed revolutionary projects. The emphasis here is on the word 'translated', for it was, of course, central to the Protestant Project of 'the priesthood of all believers' that the individual Christian should have direct access to the Word of God and that meant translating the Bible from Catholic Latin into the appropriate vernacular. One of the direct results of the availability of the translated Bible could well be a decline in respect for traditional authority, *secular* as well as *religious*. As things turned out, men and women soon discovered, in Christopher Hill's phrase, that the Bible was 'a huge bran-tub from which anything might be drawn' (Hill, 1993, p. 5). It proved to be a fund of powerful metaphors and images which helped individuals make sense of their current dilemmas and encouraged them to question the existing order of things.

In 1528, very soon after he had completed the first part of his translation of the New Testament, William Tyndale felt obliged to publish a treatise defending himself from accusations that the availability of God's Word in English 'causeth insurrection and teacheth the people to disobey . . . and moveth them to rise against their princes, and to make all things common, and to make havoc of other men's goods' (quoted in Hill, 1993, p. 3). Despite the warnings of Tyndale's enemies and the opposition of the Catholic Church, Henry VIII's Vicar-General and chief adviser Thomas Cromwell issued a decree in 1535 ordering the new English Bible to be placed in every parish church. But after his fall from power and execution in 1540, serious attempts were made to limit the social area of theological discussion. An Act of Parliament passed in 1543 was intended to prevent women (apart from noblewomen and gentlewomen), artisans, husbandmen, labourers and servants from reading or discussing the Bible. Henry VIII's prohibition proved, however, to be unworkable; and first the Government of Edward VI and then that of Elizabeth I was forced to allow free access to the scriptures in English.

Popular Bible reading, both inside and outside the home, clearly alarmed both the ecclesiastical and the secular authorities. Henry VIII complained to Parliament in 1546 that the Bible was 'disputed, rhymed, sung and jangled in every alehouse and tavern'. Elizabeth I's Archbishop of Canterbury John Whitgift could not conceal his dislike of the practice of reading and expounding the Bible in the home, especially when outsiders were present, with no university-trained divine handy to interpret 'difficult' or 'controversial' passages. And Sir John Coke, Secretary of State to Charles I, declared frankly that 'the chief use of the clergy is now the defence of our Church and therein of our State' (see Hill, 1993, pp. 15–17). The Bible in English could not be abolished; but for the century after the Reformation, the Anglican Church did its best to smother the revolutionary message which many English men and women read into it. It was essential that there should be an educated clergyman in every parish, capable of 'interpreting' the Scriptures for his flock, solving their problems and checking any heretical or subversive ideas they might harbour. It was obvious to the Church and the Government that both Biblical texts and the commentaries that usually accompanied them could be used as powerful weapons in the Puritan-radical struggle against monarchy, popery and even the established social order.

The state church attempted to restore some sort of order and control after the Restoration of Charles II in 1660; but the door which had been opened could never be shut again. The availability of the Bible in English had proved a great stimulus to learning to read; and direct access to the sacred text had caused many people to think about desirable alternatives to a hierarchical society and a hierarchical church. This was indeed a cultural revolution of unprecedented proportions, and one whose consequences stretched far beyond the period of the Reformation and the English Revolution.

In the eighteenth century, proponents of liberal political economy objected to all forms of education for the poor – and particularly Charity Schools – as dangerous and misconceived prototypes of benevolence. They took seriously the view that too much education or schooling would simply make the working poor discontented with their lot, a proposition put forward by Bernard Mandeville in *The Fable of the Bees*. This eighteenth-century cause célèbre and notorious piece of social satire by a native of Rotterdam in Holland who spent most of his adult life in London was published in its final form in 1724; and its author's views on the education of the poor were to be found in a late addition to the work called 'An Essay on Charity and Charity Schools':

> The Welfare and Felicity . . . of every State and Kingdom require that the Knowledge of the Working Poor should be confined within the Verge of their Occupations, and never extended (as to things visible) beyond what relates to their Calling. The more a Shepherd, a Plowman or any other Peasant knows of the World and of the things that are Foreign to his Labour or Employment, the less fit he'll be to go through the Fatigues and Hardships of it with Cheerfulness and Content. . . . Reading, Writing and Arithmetic are very necessary to those whose Business requires such Qualifications, but where Peoples

Livelihood has no dependence on these Arts, they are very pernicious to the Poor, who are forc'd to get their Daily Bread by their Daily Labour. Few Children make any progress at School, but, at the same time, they are capable of being employ'd in some Business or other, so that every Hour those poor People spend at their Books is so much time lost to the Society. Going to School in comparison to Working is Idleness, and the longer Boys continue in this easy sort of Life, the more unfit they'll be when grown up for downright Labour, both as to Strength and as to Inclination. For Men who are to remain and to end their Days in a Laborious, Tiresome and Painful Station of Life, the sooner they are put upon it first, the more patiently they'll submit to it for ever after. (Mandeville, 1970 edition, pp. 294–5)

The campaign for national state education in the early decades of the nineteenth century, spearheaded by the 'radical wing' of the middle class, was repeatedly thwarted in Parliament by aristocratic members of the Lords and their Tory allies in the Commons using arguments very similar to those deployed a century earlier by Bernard Mandeville. The Tory opposition case was put with great clarity by Davies Giddy in a famous speech attacking the Parochial Schools Bill, a bill for the establishment of parish schools introduced into the Commons by Samuel Whitbread, the liberal-Whig Leader, in 1807:

However specious in theory the project might be of giving education to the labouring classes of the poor, it would, in effect, be found to be prejudicial to their morals and happiness; it would teach them to despise their lot in life, instead of making them good servants in agriculture and other laborious employments to which their rank in society had destined them; instead of teaching them the virtue of subordination, it would render them factious and refractory, as is evident in the manufacturing counties; it would enable them to read seditious pamphlets, vicious books and publications against Christianity; it would render them insolent to their superiors; and, in a few years, the result would be that the legislature would find it necessary to direct the strong arm of power towards them and to furnish the executive magistrates with more vigorous powers than are now in force. Besides, if this Bill were to pass into law, it would go to burthen the country with a most enormous and incalculable expense, and to load the industrious orders with still heavier imposts. (*Hansard*, House of Commons, Vol. 9, Col. 798, 13 July 1807, quoted in Simon, 1960, p. 132; see also Green, 1990, p. 262)

So strongly were views like these held among the political elite that even Hannah More, a leading philanthropist and author of a number of influential tracts whose loyalty to Church, Monarchy and the Established Order could not be questioned, had experienced strong criticism for setting up her Sunday Schools in the Mendips mining area in the late 1790s – schools which, as far as she was concerned, had the clear political purpose of inculcating a state of resignation and obedience in the labouring classes. In defending her Schools against the charges levelled at them, she was anxious to clarify her strictly limited view of the purpose of education for the poor:

> My plan of instruction is indeed extremely simple and limited. They learn, on weekdays, such coarse works as may fit them for servants. I allow of no writing for the poor. My object is not to make them fanatics, but to train up the lower classes in habits of industry and piety. (Johnson, 1925, p. 183)

Such views were eventually challenged and defeated; and, despite its limitations and shortcomings, the Forster Education Act of 1870 was a truly radical measure in that it laid the foundations of a universal system of elementary schools for the working class. The fact that this measure was passed only three years after the Franchise Act of 1867 underlines the connection between the idea of mass popular education on the one hand and the extension of the franchise on the other. Brian Simon has pointed out that the idea of universal education had been fundamental to the thinking of the 'philosophic radicals' Jeremy Bentham and James Mill who, in the early decades of the nineteenth century, had shown no respect for the values of the landed aristocracy and had been determined to oust this class from political power:

> Education was to be the means by which the mass of the people, the 'labouring poor', would be brought to understand their clear identity of interest with the middle class. Hence the Benthamite 'democratic model', which envisaged government by Parliamentary representatives of the middle class, elected on a universal franchise by an 'educated' and so 'enlightened'

working class. By this means, the self-interested rule of the landed aristocracy would be overthrown, and a government, based on the willing franchise of the people, would be substituted. . . . The Reform Act of 1867 brought approximately a million artisans on to the voting registers and, in terms of the Benthamite creed, made universal education a political necessity. (Simon, 1965, pp. 11–12)

Central to the implementation of the 1870 Education Act were the 2500 new School Boards which, in the words of Professor Richard Aldrich, were to play a major role in 'redefining elementary education in terms of universal schooling' (Aldrich, 1982, p. 79). These ad hoc bodies were directly elected and independent of existing forms of local government. They varied in size from that of London, which had some 55 members and soon controlled nearly 400 schools, to the rural boards, many of which had only one school under their control. By the end of 1871, 117 School Boards had instituted by-laws requiring some degree of compulsory attendance. By 1900, nearly half the children who attended public elementary schools were in board schools; and in large urban areas the proportion was often much higher.

The vast scope and achievements of the London School Board made it a national institution. It erected buildings which set standards for others to emulate; it established a system of school attendance officers, known somewhat euphemistically as 'visitors', who soon provided a wealth of detailed and reliable information about the lives of the urban poor; and it appointed its own medical officer to report on air space and the ventilation of classrooms and to examine children with 'special needs'. Its debates and discussions were even reported in *The Times*, which had declared at the inception of the Board in November 1870: 'No equally powerful body will exist in England outside Parliament, if power is to be measured by influence for good or evil over masses of human beings' (*The Times*, 29 November 1870, quoted in Armytage, 1964, p. 146). Between 1871 and 1903, the number of pupils in board schools in London rose from 1117 to 549,677; while those in voluntary schools dropped from 221,401 to 213,297.[2]

In the large towns, the School Boards were often lively, progressive bodies with able and committed members who looked upon their service on the Boards as important social work. The schools they administered were regarded by many as a civilizing influence in the areas they served. Writing, for example, about the situation in an area of South London, an HMI (Her Majesty's Inspector) observed in 1882: 'Every new Board School erected in the midst of the crowded and joyless streets of Walworth or Peckham is eagerly welcomed by all the parents, and soon becomes a new centre of civilization and intelligence' (quoted in Rubinstein, 1977, p. 237). And for Sir Arthur Conan Doyle's great fictional character Sherlock Holmes, the new Board Schools – 'those big, isolated clumps of buildings rising up above the slates, like brick islands in a lead-coloured sea' – held out exciting prospects for the future. They were, in his view: 'Lighthouses . . . Beacons of the future! Capsules, with hundreds of bright little seeds in each, out of which will spring the wiser, better England of the future'.[3]

Yet although the embryonic state education system (and it was only a tentative beginning) may have been a source of pride for some contemporary observers, the reforms introduced by Forster and the developments that then ensued were viewed with alarm by many on the Right of the political spectrum. On the one hand, or so it was believed, mass education would inevitably create aspirations that society could not match; while, at the same time, the reforms clearly represented an unnecessary and costly diversion from the true path that legislators should be following, leaving education as a matter of purely *private* concern. As recently as the 1980s, the late Keith Joseph, who was Margaret Thatcher's Secretary of State for Education from 1981 to 1986, was arguing that Parliament had made a big mistake back in 1870; and that the fundamental problem with the state education system they had inaugurated lay in the very fact that it was a *state* system:

> We have a bloody state system; I wish we hadn't got one. I wish we'd taken a different route in 1870. We got the ruddy state involved. I don't want it. I don't think we know how to do it. I certainly don't think Secretaries of State know anything about it. But we are landed with it. If we could move back to 1870, I would take a different route. We've got compulsory education, which is a responsibility of hideous importance; and we tyrannize children to do that which they don't want to do, and we don't produce results. (quoted in Chitty, 1997, p. 80)

As things turned out, implementation of the 1870 Act did not, in fact, run smoothly; and a number of School Boards created problems for themselves with rival bodies and the Government by boldly determining to modify and enhance their original brief. By the end of the nineteenth century, the larger Boards had significantly altered the legislators' original concept of elementary schooling in terms of buildings, equipment, curricula and age range. In some instances, higher classes, higher tops and even separate higher grade schools were being established for older pupils who showed ability and commitment. In addition, from 1890, a new type of evening school was being developed which provided, under school board auspices, more advanced education for young persons and adults (see Aldrich, 1982, p. 83).

In June 1899 a case was brought by a School of Art in London which complained of competition from evening classes run by the London School Board. And, significantly, this institution was backed by an influential committee which had been formed to 'combat the School Boards' and, in particular, to 'undermine the advanced work' fostered by them. The judgment given in this case was of profound importance, for the District Auditor made a ruling disallowing expenditure from the rates by the London School Board towards the running of higher-grade classes in science and art. This was the famous Cockerton Judgment, which sealed the fate of advanced, or secondary, teaching fostered by the more radical and enterprising School Boards. The London School Board promptly appealed, but the judgment was upheld by the courts in December 1900. A fresh appeal was then prepared which came before the Master of the Rolls in April 1901 when the Cockerton Judgment was upheld for a second time. And all this was used to discredit the work of the School Boards as a whole and to pave the way for making the County and County Borough Councils, henceforth known as Local Education Authorities (LEAs), responsible for all types of education in their areas.

The abolition of the School Boards was one of the major provisions of the 1902 Education Act which established a clear and rigid distinction between elementary and secondary education (see Simon, 1965, pp. 208–46). From now on there was to be no confusion: two systems, each with a distinct educational and social function, were to run parallel to each other; and there was to be no place for the higher-grade schools and classes which were deemed to have strayed into the preserves of secondary and higher education. The vast majority of children were to be educated in elementary schools where they would remain until they reached the statutory school-leaving age. This was raised to fourteen by the 1918 Education Act, a measure which actually came into force in 1921. In reality, even though elementary education was free, a considerable number of children had to cease attending full-time at the age of twelve, when family circumstances made it necessary for them to seek part-time employment. It was possible for some pupils to leave the elementary school and gain admittance to a secondary school by means of a competitive system of scholarships. This was seen as promoting the concept of the 'ladder of opportunity', whereby a limited number of working-class children could be 'rescued' from their restricted lifestyle and enter a new sphere of life, not only in terms of the academic curriculum on offer but also with regard to the 'total environment' designed to form character and outlook for which grammar schools were known and widely respected.

The 1944 Education Act sought to extend educational opportunity by introducing the principle of 'free secondary education for all'; but it was a very divided system of secondary schools that emerged after the Second World War, based on the widely held belief that it was possible to say, from the results of tests administered at the age of eleven, what a child's future accomplishments would be. Those who 'passed' the new eleven-plus selection examination, roughly one in five of all children in 1950, could gain access to grammar schools; while, for the majority of those pupils who 'failed', the only school on offer was one of the new secondary moderns, dismissed by many as merely the old elementary schools writ large. And it is clear that patronizing attitudes towards the sort of education thought 'appropriate' for working-class youngsters persisted in the type of curriculum provided for most of the children attending these new secondary modern schools. In a debate in the House of Commons held in January 1965, the late Conservative politician Quintin Hogg articulated a commonly held view about the low aspirations and capabilities of secondary modern pupils when he launched a spirited attack on Labour MPs for their support of comprehensive reorganization:

> I can assure Hon. Members opposite that if they would go to study what is now being done in good secondary modern schools, they would not find a lot of pupils biting their nails in frustration because they had failed the eleven-plus. The pleasant noise of banging metal and sawing wood would greet their ears, and a smell of cooking with rather expensive equipment would come out of the front door to greet them. They would find that these boys and girls were getting an education tailor-made to their desires, their bents and their requirements. . . . I am not prepared to admit that the party opposite has done a

good service to education, or to the children of this country, by attacking that form of school, or seeking to denigrate it. (*Hansard*, House of Commons, Vol. 705, Cols 423–4, 21 January 1965)

Some of the recent contributions to the ongoing debate about the desirability or otherwise of mass education have returned to the themes that have preoccupied leading philosophers and political thinkers over the last four hundred years. In his influential book *The Meaning of Conservatism*, which was written in the late 1970s and first published in 1980, Professor Roger Scruton of Birkbeck College, London, later to become a prominent member of the 1980s right-wing education think-tank the Hillgate Group, argued forcibly that it was 'absurd' and 'unrealistic' to embrace the concept of 'equality of opportunity' in matters regarding schooling:

> Such a thing seems to be neither possible nor desirable. For what opportunity does an *unintelligent* child have to partake of the advantages conferred by an institution which demands *intelligence*? His [sic] case is no different from that of a plain girl competing with a pretty girl for a position as a model. The attempt to provide equality of opportunity, unless it is to involve massive compulsory surgery of an unthinkable kind, is simply a confused stumble in the dark. (Scruton, 1980, p. 157)

Professor Scruton went on to echo one of the main points made by Bernard Mandeville in his eighteenth-century tract *The Fable of the Bees*:

> It is simply not possible to provide universal education in any society. Nor, indeed, is it *desirable*. For the appetite for learning points people only in a certain direction; and it siphons them away from those places where they might have been contented. There are many occupations . . . which require a form of natural intelligence, and yet will not appeal to someone who has been flattered by the gift of education. It is surely important for a society that it contain as many 'walks of life' as the satisfaction of its members may require, and that it accord to each of those stations its own dignity and recompense. And it must somehow safeguard itself from future problems . . . by sustaining institutions which are *not* educational and which do not merely siphon away people to the point where they no longer wish to do what

in fact they might otherwise have done willingly and well . . . It is difficult to imagine a contented society in which every signal-box was manned by a graduate in sociology, every shop-floor directed by a philosopher and every field tilled by a barrister-at-law. It is necessary that the state should contain institutions which make contact with these occupations . . . without the adoption of some specifically *educational* purpose. (Scruton, 1980, pp. 157–8)

At the time when Roger Scruton's book was first published, there were indeed widespread fears that educational reform would bring with it social unrest and a discontented workforce. This was, after all, the period – the early 1980s – when, for reasons that were not strictly *educational* and had much to do with racial tension and mounting unemployment, there were localized but serious outbursts of rebellion among young people in (among other places) Brixton in South London, Moss Side, Manchester and the Toxteth district of Liverpool (see Young, 1989, pp. 233–4, 237–8). In interviews conducted at this time with senior DES officials and policy advisers, Professor Stewart Ranson of Birmingham University was made acutely aware of very real government fears about the imminent dangers and threats arising from 'over-education' in a contracting labour market. In a famous paper, first published in 1984, more than one DES official was shown to be quite open about the need to restrict educational opportunities for the sake of social harmony and a compliant workforce:

To offer young people advanced education, but not thereafter the work opportunities to match their career aspirations, is to offer them a false prospectus.

There has to be selection because we are beginning to create aspirations which increasingly society just cannot match. In some ways, this points to the recent success of education in contrast to the public mythology which has been created. When young people drop off the education production line and cannot find work at all, or work which meets their abilities or expectations, then we are only creating frustration with perhaps disturbing social consequences. We have to select: to ration the *educational* opportunities to meet the *job* opportunities, so that society can cope with the output of education.

We are in a period of considerable social change. There may be social unrest, but we can always cope with the Toxteths. But if we have a highly educated and *idle* population, we may possibly anticipate more serious social conflict. People must be educated once more to know their place. (Ranson, 1984, p. 241)

All the above statements, by three different individuals, emphasize the dangers of creating an 'over-educated' society and tell us a great deal about the thinking at the very heart of government in the 1970s and 1980s. Taken in conjunction with the comments of Professor Scruton, they articulate the twin related fears that large numbers of 'well-educated' youngsters will find it impossible to find work that matches their qualifications and that the jobs they do manage to acquire will simply make them feel cheated and alienated.

Conclusion

If mass education has been viewed as a 'threat' for so many centuries, it is really not difficult to understand why eugenic ideas acquired such extraordinary influence among policy-makers and bureaucrats in the first half of the twentieth century. The next chapter traces the origin of these ideas in the writings of Francis Galton and others and seeks to establish to what extent they did actually determine government policy in a number of key social areas, and particularly education.

Chapter 2

The Origins of the Eugenics Movement

Introduction

Within the space of a little over ten years in the middle of the nineteenth century, two tracts were published which were to have a profound impact worldwide and change forever existing perceptions of human development and social progress: *The Communist Manifesto*, drafted by Karl Marx and Friedrich Engels and published anonymously in London in February 1848, and *The Origin of Species*, written by Charles Darwin and published in November 1859. We know that Marx and Darwin exchanged letters and took a keen interest in each other's work. Darwin's evolutionary theories challenged the forces of tradition and conservatism, especially in matters relating to religious orthodoxy; and Marx immediately hailed the *Origin* as 'the basis in natural science for our views' (Letter from Marx to Engels, 19 December 1860, quoted in Hobsbawm, 1975, p. 305). Yet being a man of moderate liberal views, Darwin was in no sense an advocate of revolutionary social upheaval; and he politely rejected Marx's suggestion that he should be the dedicatee of the second volume of *Das Kapital*.

Marx obviously looked forward to the time when political and economic power would pass into the hands of the working class; and he saw this process being facilitated by basic flaws and contradictions within the existing capitalist system. And while Darwin shared none of Marx's revolutionary fervour, he was at least happy to accept from the late 1850s that his views encouraged a way of thinking about society as an *improvable entity*, with human beings having a new and central role in the development of their own lives. The conclusion to Darwin's 1859 treatise included the extremely optimistic statement – though, admittedly, one open to a number of different interpretations – that 'as natural selection works solely by and for the good of each being, all corporeal and mental endowments will tend to progress towards perfection' (Darwin, 1859, p.

402). An article by Darwinian scholar Julia Wedgwood called 'The Old Order Changeth' and published in *Contemporary Review* in September 1896 argued that the whole Darwinian doctrine could be 'compressed into the statement that the world was not made 6,000 years ago, but is making still' (quoted in Read, 1979, p. 296).

Yet in the years that followed the publication of *The Origin of Species*, many of Darwin's radical views were used, or rather *misused*, to support arguments that were hardly compatible with optimistic views of human progress and which saw social change as being largely governed by the harsh rules of biological evolution. It was now argued that where the development of human personality was concerned, *nature* was more important than *nurture* and *heredity* was more important than *environment*, itself a term capable of many different meanings and embracing a number of qualitatively varied influences, both natural and social. Darwin's theory that the process of 'natural selection' had been responsible for the 'superiority' of human beings was now extended to support the view that natural selection had also determined the fact that some human beings were obviously innately 'superior' to others. Ideas that initially appealed chiefly to socialists and social democrats were also to be taken up by a number of right-wing philosophers and political thinkers who contemplated the possibility that natural selection could well produce a new race or class of 'superior beings', destined to dominate their 'human inferiors' in much the same way that human beings dominated and exploited members of the animal kingdom.

Those who sought to apply Darwinian principles to their analysis of the human condition actually differed in their views as to whether or not the state had a role to play in creating the sort of society they wished to live in. The English philosopher Herbert Spencer (1820–1903), who coined the phrase 'survival of the fittest' in his work *Social Statics* published in 1851 (eight years before the first appearance of *The Origin of Species*), believed passionately in the non-interference of the state in all areas of social policy. Yet the very phrase 'survival of the fittest' was regarded by many as being bland in the extreme, meaning no more than that those who survive are fit and those who are fit survive. Leading Social Darwinians like Benjamin Kidd and Karl Pearson rejected Spencer's notion of 'laissez-faire individualism' because it failed to acknowledge that interference with individual life was necessary in the name of racial improvement or survival.

It was, above all, Darwin's second cousin, explorer and scientist Francis Galton (1822–1911), who sought to provide 'scientific' justification for a whole series of projects designed to maintain and, where possible, improve the genetic condition of the human race. Galton was particularly concerned to ensure that 'racial purity' should not be undermined in increasingly democratic and egalitarian societies where the average level of ability and creativity might be in danger of declining as a result of those at the bottom end of the social scale 'over breeding'. Whereas, for Marx and Darwin, current social developments could be said to represent progress and achievement, for Galton, the very idea of increasing working-class numbers and influence had frightening implications. In seeking to clarify the principles of what came to be known as Social Darwinism, Galton was also concerned to establish psychology as a *biological* science. In his first book on the subject, *Hereditary Genius*, which appeared in 1869, he published the results of a major genealogical study of scientific families, claiming thereby to demonstrate that 'genius' was inborn and confined almost exclusively to certain types of privileged families with innate qualities and abilities. In this work, he also extolled the virtues of 'judicious marriages', lamenting 'the degradation of human nature' by 'the propagation of the unfit' and invoking the duty of the leaders of society to avoid certain disaster by arguing for the enforcement or at least encouragement of clearly defined breeding policies. Fourteen years later, he coined the term 'eugenics' – now commonly defined as the study of methods of improving the innate quality of the human race, especially by selective breeding – in the first edition of *Inquiries into Human Faculty and its Development*, published in 1883. For Galton, the term was apposite because it came from the Greek word *eugenēs* which was used to describe someone who was hereditarily endowed with noble qualities. In the years that followed, Galton always defined eugenics as the science which deals with all the influences that both preserve the inborn qualities of a race and, at the same time, develop them to the utmost advantage.

Some of Darwin's disciples challenged the thinking of the eugenicists. T. H. Huxley, for example, emphasized in an important article called 'The Struggle for Existence', published in *Fortnightly Review* in February 1888, and in his 1893 Romanes Lecture on *Evolution and Ethics* that Darwin's theory of natural selection should *not* be used to justify a competitive free-for-all in human society. In Huxley's view, the natural process must always be controlled by rational and ethical thinking. The 1893 Lecture argued that 'right social conduct' required self-restraint: 'in place of thrusting aside, or treading down all competitors, it requires that the individual shall not merely respect, but shall help his fellows'. Social policy should be directed 'not so much to the survival of the fittest, as to the fitting of as many as possible to survive'. It should repudiate 'the gladiatorial theory of existence'. By definition, contended Huxley, the establishment of human society implied the setting of clear limits; and the more complex that society became, the more would the state need to intervene for the sake of the common good. In particular, increased foreign competition in trade required sanitary reform to create 'a healthy environment', together with improved educational and recreational facilities to enhance 'the mental quality of the workforce' (quoted in Read, 1979, p. 296).

Yet despite the broad appeal of Huxley's thinking among social reformers, it was Galton, Kidd and Pearson who constituted the dominant force among Darwin's disciples in the closing decades of the nineteenth century. Of these men, Galton exerted the chief influence; and it would seem appropriate to devote the next section of this chapter to a detailed account of his life and writings.

The Life and Career of Francis Galton

Often described as a great Victorian polymath, Francis Galton made lasting contributions in fields as diverse as African exploration, geography, meteorology, statistics, psychology, personal identification and human heredity. He has been the subject of just *four* biographies, two of them produced since the start of this century. The first of these accounts of Galton's life and work – and the most reverential – was an early four-volume 'labour of love', written by his ardent disciple Karl Pearson and published between 1914 and 1930 (Pearson, 1914; 1924; 1930). The second, with the title *Francis Galton: The Life and Work of a Victorian Genius*, was written by D. W. Forrest and published in 1974 (Forrest, 1974). The third of these biographies – and the first to place Galton clearly in the age to which he belonged – was written by the American geneticist and Professor of Biology Nicholas Wright Gillham and published in 2001 (Gillham, 2001). And the most recent account – and in many ways the most critical and unorthodox – had the title *Extreme Measures: The Dark Visions and Bright Ideas of Francis Galton* and was written by Martin Brookes and published in 2004 (Brookes, 2004).[1]

Broadly speaking, Galton's research and published writings concentrated on two distinct sets of problems; and his life can be divided rather neatly into two main parts. During the first part of his career, lasting down to around 1860, he was engaged chiefly in exploration and the study of geography. Travel writing related to this interest, as did a concern with meteorology, and he is credited with the discovery of the anticyclone. The second part of his career was devoted to the issues surrounding human heredity. To investigate the heritability of what Galton referred to as 'talent and character' at a time when IQ tests had not been developed, Galton used pedigrees, twin studies and anthropometric measurements. He invented new statistical tools to facilitate the analysis of the masses of data he accumulated. As Professor Gillham has pointed out, 'he believed that favourable physical characteristics correlated with superior mental qualities, but he had no way to compare these directly. Consequently, he ventured into areas of psychology and personal identification, eventually lighting upon fingerprinting as a foolproof way to distinguish individuals' (Gillham, 2001, p. 3).

Galton was born in 1822 into a prosperous Midlands family, his father being at one time High Bailiff of Birmingham and later, following his retirement from banking, a magistrate and deputy lieutenant in Leamington in Warwickshire. Francis was the grandson of the eminent physician and inventor Erasmus Darwin, thereby, in Gillham's words (and assuming one shares Galton's own views on the importance of such things), 'deriving all the benefits of an enviable pedigree',[2] and the second cousin of Charles Darwin, who was thirteen years his senior. He was regarded as being a precocious child, having apparently memorized the six thousand lines of Sir Walter Scott's epic poem *Marmion* by the time he reached the age of five.

It was originally intended that the young Galton should embark on a career in medicine. Yet while studying the subject at King's College in London in the academic year of 1839–40, he became friendly with his cousin Charles who was living nearby on Upper Gower Street. And under Darwin's influence, Galton convinced his father to send him to Trinity College, Cambridge to study mathematics. The usual course of medical study required four years. When he made his decision to switch to mathematics, Galton already had two under his belt, having spent the academic year 1838–39 serving as an apprentice at the General Hospital in Birmingham, but he was still only seventeen and could not qualify for the Degree of Bachelor of Medicine until he was 21. In his letters to his indulgent father, he argued that a period at Cambridge studying mathematics still would be exciting and advantageous and enable him to return to his medical studies immediately afterwards to qualify for the Degree with his medical courses fresh in his mind. In fact, Galton was frequently ill during his time at Cambridge and he failed to graduate with honours in mathematics, even though his enthusiasm for analysing all scientific problems *quantitatively* remained undimmed. And this was to be the unifying thread that ran throughout his life and career, causing Martin Brookes to argue that many of his experiments seemed to involve 'measuring for measuring's sake: the product of an obsessive drive he possessed from childhood' (Brookes, 2004, p. xiv).

Galton never, in fact, resumed his medical studies at King's College when he came down from Cambridge in 1844. All professional and academic aspirations were set aside in October of that year when his father's death relieved Francis of any financial worries, and he was now young and wealthy enough to indulge his passion for travel and adventure. For the next six years – referred to by Karl Pearson as 'six fallow years' and by Professor Gillham as 'Galton's rudderless period' – his life appeared to lack all sense of purpose and direction, but then, in 1850–2, he spent two eventful years in Africa, mounting at his own expense a major expedition to what is today northern Namibia but was then the uncharted domain of the warring Damara and Namaqua peoples. By all accounts, he proved a brave and resourceful leader, and he returned to England in April 1852 to great acclaim, receiving the Royal Geographical Society's Founder's Medal in 1853 and being elected a Fellow of the Royal Society, at the comparatively young age of 34, in 1856. Being in every sense politically and socially conservative, Galton was proud to be a traditionalist who always paid due deference to establishment norms and values. After 1856, he quickly became a member of the scientific elite, presiding, for example, as a senior committee member of the RGS over the heated controversies surrounding the discovery of the source(s) of the Nile and Stanley's rescue of Livingstone.

It was at this period in his life that Galton published two popular and influential books: *Tropical South Africa* in 1853 and *The Art of Travel* in 1855. The first of these books provided many examples of Galton's crude and patronising attitudes towards 'race' and so-called primitive behaviour. Throughout the text, Galton aired his lofty views on the local African people that he had met on his travels. As Martin Brookes has pointed out, 'these were not carefully considered anthropological insights or deft illustrations of cultural contrasts. They often involved vicious, racist rhetoric' (Brookes, 2004, p. 112). Galton's account of his first meeting with the Nama tribesmen at Walfisch Bay set the tone of the book: 'I found that some had trousers, some coats of skin, and they clicked, and howled, and chattered, and generally behaved like baboons. I looked on all these fellows as a sort of primitive link with civilization'. And Galton also provided an ongoing ridicule of the Damara people's character, customs and culture, arguing that: 'There is hardly a particle of romance, or affection, or poetry in their character or creed; but they are a greedy, heartless silly set of savages' (ibid., pp. 112–13). At another point in the narrative, he complained bitterly that the Damara language had, as he put it, 'no numeral greater than three':

> Once, while I watched a poor Damara floundering hopelessly over a large number in a calculation on one side of me, I observed Dinah, my spaniel, equally embarrassed on the other. She was overlooking half a dozen of her new-born puppies, which had been removed two or three times from her, and her anxiety was excessive, as she tried to find out if they were all present, or if any were still missing. She kept puzzling and running her eyes over them backwards and forwards, but could not satisfy herself. She evidently did have a vague notion of counting, even though the figure was too large for her brain. Yet taking the two as they stood, dog and Damara, the comparison reflected no great honour on the man. (quoted in Gillham, 2001, p. 80)

Such observations come across to a twenty-first-century reader as both insulting and pointless. Yet it is quite likely that Galton's Victorian audience would have found nothing to complain about. For even though Britain had abolished slavery in 1833, Galton's assessment of all African peoples as generally primitive and uncultured merely reflected the racist consensus then prevalent throughout the country.

For Francis Galton at the age of 37, it was the publication of Charles Darwin's *The Origin of Species* in November 1859 that marked a turning point in his life and in his view of its ultimate purpose and direction. In his own words, 'it made a marked epoch in my own mental development, as it did in human thought generally' (quoted in Gillham, 2001, p. 155). He was now determined to devote his life to the study of what he saw as the central topics of heredity and the improvement of the human race. From the outset, he was convinced that *nature* and not *nurture* determined human ability. Indeed, the very phrase 'nature and nurture' is one he coined himself, first using it as the subtitle of his 1875 work *English Men of Science: Their Nature and Nurture*. The means of proving his theory was to be 'pedigree analysis', a fairly straightforward device that was to remain an analytical mainstay for over 40 years. He reasoned that if 'eminence' (or at least 'superior ability') was heritable, then a great man's closest male relatives were the most likely to exhibit exceptional qualities. Qualitative information could be converted to numerical data by making the simple assumption that a man was either 'eminent' or he was not. It needs to be emphasized that women played no part in Galton's research because, as Professor Gillham points out, 'his Victorian mindset viewed notable achievement as principally a *male* prerogative' (ibid.).

The key themes of Galton's work in the second half of his life were established at the outset in two articles entitled 'Hereditary Talent and Character', published in *Macmillan's Magazine* in June and August 1865. This was a prestigious journal of the period, and Galton could expect to have a wide and discerning audience for his views. It was here that he first set out to prove that Darwin's theory of 'natural selection' should not be restricted to the breeding of domestic animals and cultivated plants. What was true of the breeding process in animals was equally true of the way human beings developed. But obviously things could not be left to chance. Selective breeding should be used for the purpose of promoting one class or race of humans with superior qualities while, at the same time, discouraging the propagation of other groups with less desirable traits. It seems that Galton was particularly impressed by a key passage in Darwin's 1859 text which stated that:

> We cannot suppose that all breeds of animal were suddenly produced as perfect and as useful as we now see them; indeed, in many cases, we know that this has not been their history. The key is man's power of accumulative selection: nature gives successive variations; man adds them up in certain directions useful to him. In this sense, he may be said to have made for himself useful breeds. (Darwin, 1859, p. 21)

As we have already noted earlier in this chapter, it was in his book *Hereditary Genius,* published in 1869, that Galton was able to

make full use of 'pedigree analysis' to demonstrate to his own satisfaction the inheritance of 'talent and character'. On the very first
page of the work, he declared his intention:

> to show in this book that a man's natural abilities are derived
> by inheritance, under exactly the same limitations as are the
> form and physical features of the whole organic world.
> Consequently, as it is easy, notwithstanding those limitations, to
> obtain by careful selection a permanent breed of dogs or horses
> gifted with the peculiar powers of running, or of doing anything
> else, so it would be quite practicable to produce a highly gifted
> race of men by judicious marriage during several consecutive
> generations. I shall show that some social agencies of an
> ordinary character, whose influences are little suspected, are at
> this moment working towards the degradation of human nature,
> and that others are working towards its improvement. I
> conclude that each generation has enormous power over the
> natural gifts of those that follow, and maintain that it is a duty
> we owe to humanity to investigate the range of that power, and
> to exercise it in a way that, without being unwise towards
> ourselves, shall be most advantageous to future inhabitants of
> the earth. (Galton, 1869, p. 1)

Clearly the 'degradation of human nature', referred to above, was
being brought about by the propagation of 'the unfit' and 'the
feebleminded', but, at this stage in his output, Galton was not very
clear as to what should be done about it. He was beginning to
develop the concepts of what would later become 'positive' and
'negative' eugenics, but they were not worked out in detail and,
throughout the period from 1865 to 1911, he was not precise
about the power that should be wielded by the central government.
One factor he was already convinced exerted a powerful influence
in determining the health and virility of the population centred on
the average age of marriage. Since those marrying young had the
larger families, produced more generations within a given period of
time and ensured that more generations were alive at the same
time, the wisest policy for any society to follow was one that
resulted in 'retarding the average age of marriage among the weak,
and in hastening it among the vigorous classes' (Galton, 1869, pp.
406–7).

What Galton was really determined to prove in *Hereditary Genius*
was the inheritability of mental ability. And he was able to report

that the 300 distinguished families he had studied for his research contained nearly 1000 eminent men; compared to the frequency of one eminent man in 4000 he estimated for the population as a whole. Furthermore, the closer the kinship to the eminent man, the higher the probability of distinction. He acknowledged that his critics would argue that nurture could also play a role, since 'the son of a great man will be placed in a more favourable position for advancement, than if he had been the son of an ordinary person'; but he dismissed this idea as holding true in only a very small number of cases (Galton, 1869, pp. 53, 373). And all Galton's carefully tabulated statistics underpinned the idea reiterated in one of the final chapters of the book – 'Influences that Affect the Natural Ability of Nations' – that in Britain and throughout the world, it would never be desirable for the 'superior' races and classes to put off the period of marriage until middle age or opt for small families. In Galton's words:

> I protest against the abler races being encouraged to withdraw ... from the struggle for existence. It may seem monstrous to some that the weak should be crowded out by the strong; but it is still more monstrous that the races best fitted to play their part on the stage of life should be crowded out by the incompetent, the ailing and the desponding. . . . The time may hereafter arrive, in far distant years, when the population of the earth shall be kept as strictly within the bounds of number and suitability of race as the sheep on a well-ordered moor or the plants in an orchard-house; in the meantime, let us do what we can to encourage the multiplication of the races best fitted to invent and conform to a high and generous civilization. (Galton, 1869, p. 410)

There was a varied response to Galton's dogmatic assertions in the review articles which appeared in British newspapers and periodicals (see Gillham, 2001, pp. 169–72; Brookes, 2004, pp. 167–9). Yet while the reaction to Galton's central thesis could hardly be described as universally favourable, it was at least clear that the book had succeeded in creating a stir: for a six-month period around the Christmas of 1869, the leading journals were full of serious critiques and counter-arguments. Generally speaking, while many of the book's reviewers complimented Galton on his painstaking research and striking originality, most argued that he had overstated his hereditarian case. The conclusion of *The Times* was typical of the prevailing mood: 'Mr Galton is a little too anxious to arrange all things in the wedding garment of his theory, and will scarcely allow them a stitch of other clothing.'. The writer in *The Saturday Review* took Galton to task for having 'bestowed immense pains upon the empirical proof of a thesis which from its intrinsic nature can never be proved empirically.' He went on: 'the long array of names and figures which are made to prop up the hypothesis of hereditary genius, however interesting as bits of biography, seems to us to be logically worth nothing. . . . The problem for all of us is to distinguish the elemental germ of mental difference among the mass of elements of an external kind among which it has its life and growth. . . . How can we tease apart and measure internal and external influences, when human life requires the united efforts of both for its proper development?' Writing in *The Edinburgh Review*, the leading political economist Herman Merivale identified what was probably the central weakness in Galton's thesis. Using the chapter on judges to make his case, Merivale noted that around 100 of the 125 eminent relatives of judges tabulated by Galton were also lawyers. In Merivale's view, this had little to do with 'the inheritance of a special talent of the lawyer, but much to do with the ability of a judge to influence his son to enter a legal career'. And the long review in *Chamber's Journal* made the astute observation that the very title of Galton's book was itself misleading since the author was really talking about high ability and talent. Galton himself acknowledged his mistake in the Preface to the 1892 edition of his book: 'The fault in this volume that I chiefly regret is the choice of its title of *Hereditary Genius*, but it cannot be remedied now. There was not the slightest intention on my part to use the word "genius" in any technical sense, but merely as expressing an ability that was exceptionally high and, at the same time, inborn' (pp. 25–6).[3]

Among the many letters that Galton received about his book were two from Emily Shirreff, a leading pioneer in the cause of women's education in Great Britain. She wrote fervently of the problems caused by ambitious women of 'high ability' who rejected the state of marriage in order to pursue a useful career: 'Fathers suppose that most of their daughters are willing to live in idleness until a husband takes them off their hands . . . while the abler, the more energetic, the most fit to be the mothers of a better generation will revolt against the injustice of our social arrangements, and struggle singly for an independent position; thereby sacrificing at once the interests of society and some of the highest cravings of their own nature'. Emily Shirreff was here making a key point that was to feature prominently in the eugenics literature of the early twentieth century. Because they were single-minded and ambitious, the fittest women rejected or postponed marriage in favour of a demanding career, thereby leaving production of the next generation to women who were 'poorly endowed' intellectually.

Galton understood the problem that Emily Shirreff was outlining, but the promotion of early marriage among the country's intellectual elite, with the lower orders being encouraged to have very few if any children, remained his principal plan for securing the future wellbeing of the nation – even though he came to realize that, without a supporting structure of suitable rewards and punishments, it would be very difficult to secure the co-operation of all groups and classes. Something more *dirigiste* was obviously necessary; and by the time he coined the term 'eugenics' in his 1883 book *Inquiries into Human Faculty and its Development* (Galton, 1883, p. 17), he had begun to put forward strategies of a more detailed nature for achieving his racial objectives.[4] His main idea was that schoolmasters, church ministers and doctors should be asked to assist in the collection of detailed pedigree data on the young male population of the country. Eventually, all schoolboys would be classified according to their natural gifts, both mental and physical, and special inquiries would be made into the genealogies of those who were deemed to be 'hereditarily remarkable'. It was Galton's fervent hope that, with the passage of time, families of good breeding, with sons capable of living up to their parents' expectations, would multiply rapidly, while those at the bottom end of the social scale would be encouraged to wither away. The inferior classes, and especially those showing signs of physical or mental weakness, would be expected to remain celibate, being treated 'with all kindness' by their social superiors, provided they did so. Should they procreate, the time would probably come when they would forfeit all claims to 'kindness' and have to be regarded as 'enemies of the State'.

From the above, it can be seen that, even after several years of study and research, much of Galton's thinking on ways of achieving his racial goals was still rather vague and only in embryonic form. In particular, where the problem of 'the propagation of the unfit' was concerned, it was left to his more ardent disciples to talk in terms of 'segregation' and 'voluntary' or 'compulsory sterilization'.

Galton's Legacy in America and Europe

Fixed to the wall just in front of the altar in Claverdon Church in Warwickshire[5] is a memorial to Francis Galton which reads: 'Many branches of Science owe much to his labours, but the dominant idea of his life's work was to measure the influence of heredity on the mental and physical attributes of mankind.' These words do polite justice to Galton's career, but, not surprisingly, they give little indication of the enormous power and influence, often of a malign nature, that Galton wielded wherever he went, inspiring a solid group of admirers who could be found carrying on his work long after his death in 1911. They also say nothing about the more extreme aspects of his eugenic vision and about his dream of a future society dominated by the racially pure. As I have argued elsewhere (Chitty, 2004, p. 81), 'Francis Galton is often seen as one of the evil spirits of the nineteenth century, condemning succeeding generations of psychologists to pursue a sterile debate between the absurd extremes of environmental and genetic determinism and inspiring ideas and policies which would cause misery and cruelty to millions of people in the century to come.' His biographer Martin Brookes has argued that he was indeed a man of prodigious energy and achievements, while, at the same time, conceding that his work on hereditary determinism was invariably influenced by the less attractive aspects of his personality: 'an immense snob, perennially preoccupied with distinctions of race, class and social status, Galton was routinely dismissive of those he considered beneath him – women, black people and the poor' (Brookes, 2004, p. xiv). It is also Brookes's view that, while it may be unfair and inappropriate to lay the blame at Galton's door for 'the appalling tragedy of the Holocaust', it can at least be argued that 'he was a significant contributor to what was admittedly a complex chain of events. Apart from his hereditary obsession, he was a moral relativist with a very weak faith in democracy. On occasion, his descriptions of eugenics sound uncannily prophetic of Hitler's National Socialism' (ibid., p. 297). Nicholas Gillham has taken issue with this point of view, arguing that 'Galton would have been horrified had he known that, within little more than twenty years of his death, forcible sterilization and murder would be carried out in the name of eugenics, for he was not a mean or vindictive man' (Gillham, 2001, p. 357). Yet this is not an easy matter to resolve; and reviewing Gillham's biography in *London Review of Books* (4 December 2003), Andrew Berry has argued that Galton cannot entirely escape responsibility for the ways in which subsequent generations have interpreted his pernicious theories and attempted to put them into practice (Berry, 2003, p. 23).

It is certainly true that Galton's vision of a genetic utopia acquired all manner of sinister connotations in the first half of the twentieth century as his followers organized conferences and seminars to publicize his theories. At the end of July 1912, just eighteen months after his death, the First International Congress of Eugenics was held at the Hotel Cecil in London with an impressive list of biologists, physicians and politicians from Britain, Europe and America among the principal speakers and guests.[6] It was organized by the Eugenics Education Society, which had been founded in November 1907, and given maximum publicity in the Society's journal, the *Eugenics Review*. The principal guest at the inaugural banquet was former Prime Minister Arthur Balfour who gave a speech to toast 'our foreign friends and guests'; and among the 500 or so in attendance were the Lord Mayor of London, the American Ambassador, Winston Churchill, First Lord of the Admiralty, and Alexander Graham Bell, inventor of the telephone. The Congress was to be divided into four main sections: Biology and Eugenics, Practical Eugenics, Sociology and Eugenics and Medicine and Eugenics. They were to meet sequentially on separate days so that there would be no concurrent sessions, with the English, French, German and Italian languages being used on an equal footing. All the standard worries of the eugenicists were aired by one speaker after another in the course of the six-day programme. Western civilization was in danger of collapse, since we were preserving the weak and the 'genetically undesirable' and allowing them to breed at an alarming rate. Indeed the pauper pedigrees presented at the Congress, featuring the heritability of undesirable traits among the dregs of society, proved conclusively that the poor and feeble-minded were highly fecund and would one day inherit the earth unless wise men intervened with a programme of genetic measures. On the final day of the Congress, Major Leonard Darwin, one of Charles Darwin's surviving sons, gave his President's Farewell Address in which he urged all present to return to their home countries determined to campaign for legislation designed 'to stamp out "feeblemindedness" from future generations'.

It was, in fact, in parts of America that eugenic campaigns appeared to make early progress. And here the targets included not only the poor and feebleminded, but also immigrants arriving in masses from southern and eastern Europe. In 1907, the state of

Indiana introduced the world's first compulsory sterilization law for so-called inferior beings. By 1913, 16 states had similar statutes; and by 1926, this number had increased to 23. The label of 'social degeneracy' was, of course, a conveniently loose umbrella term that afforded ample scope for all manner of prejudiced interpretations. It was normally criminals, the mentally ill and the insane who were lined up to be sterilized, but in some states, the category of 'genetic inferiority' was extended to embrace homosexuals and communists.[7]

In April 1927, the most significant case in sterilization history was argued before the US Supreme Court in the famous *Buck* v. *Bell* hearing. This involved a 'feebleminded' woman from Virginia named Carrie Buck whose mother and illegitimate daughter were also purported to be both 'feebleminded' and 'morally delinquent'. Harry H. Laughlin, Superintendent of the Eugenics Record Office, was the expert witness, and the Court finally voted eight to one in favour of compulsory sterilization, with Justice Oliver Wendell Holmes writing the majority opinion which contained the remarkable declaration that 'three generations of imbeciles are enough' and that it was quite legitimate for the state to take action to prevent 'the reproduction of degenerates'. Carrie Buck was duly sterilized; and this famous decision provided a rationale at the federal level for a practice that had already been legalized by many state legislatures (see King, 1999, p. 65).

Generally speaking Catholic countries in Europe (along with Catholic states in America) refused to contemplate any type of eugenic solution to the social and medical problems of the period. Where Britain was concerned, Galton's legacy could chiefly be found in the campaign to introduce voluntary sterilization of the mentally unfit and in the widespread use of IQ (intelligence quotient) tests for the purpose of selecting children for different types of secondary school at the age of eleven; and these issues are dealt with at some length in Chapters 3 and 4. In order to find European examples of enthusiastic and systematic application of Galton's theories to the problems posed by 'hereditary degeneracy', we have to look at the policies pursued by Switzerland, Scandinavia and Germany.

Sterilization laws of one kind or another were passed by Switzerland in 1928, by Denmark in 1929, by Norway in 1934 and by Sweden in 1935. 6000 Danes were forcibly sterilized and no fewer than 40,000 Norwegians. Even more remarkably, nearly 63,000 sterilizations were performed in Sweden between 1935 and

1975. In 1944 a law was passed in Sweden that made education for the feebleminded compulsory; but this special tuition invariably meant residence at a specified institution and separate legislation made sterilization a condition for discharge (see Areschoug, 2005). All this may come as something of a surprise to those accustomed to think of Sweden as a model social democratic state pursuing liberal and progressive social and educational policies. And Professor Richard J. Evans has attempted to provide a balanced perspective on the issue by pointing out that Swedish sterilizations were carried out to remove 'non-productive people from the chain of heredity' and that Swedish legislation targeted the *socially* rather than the *racially* deviant, so that, strictly speaking, the whole programme was not *racially* based in the way favoured by Nazi and Fascist politicians (Evans, 2005, p. 514). This being so, it is still true that the Swedish National Institute for Racial Biology did establish physical characteristics among the criteria for forcible sterilization and that gypsies were regularly targeted as a supposedly racially inferior group.

It was, of course, in Nazi Germany that Galton's ideas of racial hygiene were embraced with the most extreme enthusiasm and dogmatic zeal. Yet it is important to point out that theories of racial superiority did not suddenly acquire prominence when Adolf Hitler became German Chancellor in January 1933. Professor Ian Kershaw has argued convincingly in the first volume of his authoritative biography of Adolf Hitler both that the equation of National Socialism with Hitler has always been 'a quite misleading oversimplification' and that many of the ideas associated with Nazi ideology were in circulation in parts of Europe from the late nineteenth century onwards.

> Much of the pot-pourri of ideas that went to make up Nazi ideology – an amalgam of prejudices, phobias and utopian social expectations, rather than a coherent set of intellectual propositions – was to be found in different forms and intensities before the First World War, and later in the programmes and manifestos of the Fascist Parties of many European countries. Integral nationalism, anti-Marxist 'National' Socialism, Social Darwinism, racism, biological anti-Semitism, eugenics and elitism all intermingled in varying strengths to provide a heady brew of irrationalism attractive to some cultural pessimists among the intelligentsia and bourgeoisie of European societies undergoing rapid social, economic and political change in the

late nineteenth century. There was nothing especially Teutonic about them, though . . . some of the ideas took on a particular form and developed a specific intonation in Germany and German-speaking Austria. (Kershaw, 1998, pp. 134–5)

It is also important to note that in the early years of the Weimar Republic (1919–33), the promotion of 'racial hygiene' could mean primarily segregating or sterilizing those who were deemed *socially* or *medically* unfit; and a number of prominent Jewish doctors were, in fact, among the most enthusiastic eugenicists of the period. It was only later, in the 1930s, that eugenic solutions became inextricably linked with measures that were directly anti-Semitic. Even in the early years of the Third Reich, the people who were being sterilized were overwhelmingly 'Aryan' Germans, and they were being sterilized for reasons not very different from those being put forward by politicians and eugenicists in Sweden at around the same time.

Of all those who argued for eugenic sterilization during the Weimar Republic, two of the most prominent campaigners were Gerhard Boeters and Alfred Ploetz. A health officer in Zwickau, Boeters was strongly in favour of including 'habitual criminals' in the list of those to be sterilized. He continued to argue that such criminals had to be removed from the chain of heredity as a matter of urgency, even though it was pointed out, even by some of his fellow eugenicists, that it was not always possible to separate 'hereditarily determined criminality' cleanly from 'environmentally conditioned deviance'. Ploetz was, for many years, President of the Gesellschaft für Rassen Hygiene (Society for Racial Hygiene), the German equivalent of the English Eugenics Education Society, and he had played a leading role at the First International Congress of Eugenics held in 1912. Throughout the 1920s, he urged the Government to adopt social policies that put the improvement of the race at the top of the agenda and dealt effectively with all those who could be identified as weak, idle, criminal, degenerate and insane. In July 1932, shortly before the collapse of the Weimar Republic, the Gesellschaft für Rassen Hygiene and sections of the medical community drafted a law permitting the *voluntary* sterilization of certain classes of individuals perceived as being *hereditarily* defective, but the proposed measure required proof that the defective trails had a *genetic* basis. Confident that, with the coming of the Third Reich, such a proposal would soon receive the blessing of the Government, Ploetz wrote personally to Hitler in April 1933 explaining that, since he was now in his early seventies, he was too old to take a leading part in the practical implementation of the principles of racial hygiene, but emphasizing that he gave his whole-hearted backing to the Reich Chancellor's policies all the same (see Evans, 2005, p. 507).[8]

Such confidence was not misplaced; and practical policies were not long in coming. Indeed, the draft measure of 1932 was considered too tentative and moderate by the incoming Nazi Government, and there was to be nothing 'voluntary' about the legislation of 1933. At the beginning of the Third Reich, Interior Minister Wilhelm Frick announced that the new regime was going to concentrate public spending on racially sound and healthy people. It was not only going to reduce expenditure on 'inferior and asocial individuals, the sick, the mentally deficient, the insane, cripples and criminals'; it was also going to subject them to a ruthless policy of 'selection and eradication'. This new policy took legislative form in the 'Law for the Prevention of Hereditarily Diseased Offspring' (Gesetz zur Verhütung Erbkranken Nachwuchses), approved by the Cabinet on 14 July 1933. This prescribed *compulsory* sterilization for anyone who could be said to be suffering from one or other of a number of conditions: congenital feeblemindedness, schizophrenia, manic-depressive psychosis, hereditary epilepsy, Huntingdon's chorea, hereditary deafness, blindness or other severe physical deformity, and severe alcoholism.

The new Law was to be administered by Hereditary Health Courts and their appellate counterparts. The Appeal Courts would be presided over by a lawyer and two doctors, one of whom would be an 'expert' on genetic pathology. Some people agreed to be sterilized, but most did not. In 1934, the first year of the Law's operation, nearly 4000 people appealed against the ruling of the sterilization authorities, and 3559 of the appeals failed. In each of the first four years of the Law's operation, over 50,000 people underwent forced sterilization; and by the end of the Third Reich, around 400,000 people had been sterilized, almost all of them being operated on before the outbreak of war in September 1939.

A flurry of legislative activity concerned with eugenic matters was capped by the three notorious Nuremberg Laws of 1935, designed primarily to 'cleanse' the German population of all unwanted elements. The first two were aimed chiefly at the Jews, disenfranchising them as 'citizens', redesignating them as 'residents' and placing severe restrictions on the amount of Jewish blood permissible in interracial marriages with 'Aryan' Germans. The third Law required a premarital medical examination for the prospective husband and wife to see if 'racial damage' could result from the marriage. It also prevented marriage of individuals having presumptive 'genetic infirmities' like 'feeblemindedness'.

A very interesting example of an experiment in 'positive' eugenics was the so-called 'Lebensborn' Programme set up by SS Leader Heinrich Himmler shortly after the Nazi Party gained power.[9] Between 1935 and 1945, around 8000 German children acquired the special status of being 'Lebensborn' children, the German word being roughly translated as 'well' or 'fountain of life'. These children were the products of a bizarre Nazi breeding project, whereby SS officers would sleep with carefully selected blonde-haired, blue-eyed women (often from Scandinavia) in order to produce perfect offspring for 'the master race'. They were normally brought up in 'Lebensborn' children's homes where only those without faults or blemishes were permitted to survive. It is interesting to note, as Professor Evans has pointed out, that illegitimacy, a persistent stigma in socially and morally conservative circles, was wholly irrelevant to the Nazi view of childbirth. 'If an infant was racially pure and healthy, it did not matter at all whether its parents were legally married' (Evans, 2005, p. 521).

It was, of course, in the concentration camps that experimentation of a racial and eugenic kind assumed its most obscene form. Groups within the Nazi medical world, aided and abetted by Himmler and the SS, subjected camp inmates to various forms of 'medical' research, without first securing consent and with no regard for suffering and risk of life. Not that all the 'experiments' could even by justified, if that is the right word, on the grounds of promoting scientific and medical understanding. As John Cornwell has pointed out, 'Nazi scientists who exploited concentration camp inmates for their potential as human guinea pigs were guilty not only of blatant disregard for ethical norms of medical experiments on humans, but were also invariably involved in inflicting sadistic injury with no possible scientific purpose in view' (Cornwell, 2003, p. 357).

It was the camp at Auschwitz with its large number of 'lives not worth living' that afforded the greatest opportunities to members of the racial hygiene movement eager to carry out experiments of a eugenic nature. In the words of Laurence Rees: 'for the doctor ambitious to pursue a career in research and unencumbered by humanity or compassion, Auschwitz was a laboratory without parallel' (Rees, 2005, p. 186). And it was here that in March 1943,

Josef Mengele became Chief Medical Officer after military service on the eastern front. At Auschwitz, Mengele could do to human beings whatever he liked: there was to be no restriction on the scope or extent of his medical experiments. He worked closely with Professor Otmar von Verschuer, Director from 1942 of the Kaiser Wilhelm Institute for Anthropology, Human Genetics and Eugenics, and his main experiments were performed on dwarfs, physically deformed individuals and twins. His studies of twins which took up so much of his time were, he claimed, motivated by the desire to understand the role of genetic inheritance in human development and behaviour – the topic that obsessed all eugenicists.

This, then, was Francis Galton's legacy in America and parts of Europe, described even by Professor Gillham as 'malign' and 'much worse than anything Galton himself could have envisioned' (Gillham, 2001, pp. 2, 356). It is, of course, true that the barbaric nature of Nazi 'eugenic' policies, culminating in the Final Solution and the Holocaust, led to a total revulsion against the 'pseudo-science' of eugenics at the end of the Second World War when the extent of the killing in the death camps became apparent. Nevertheless, eugenic sterilizations continued to be carried out from time to time in parts of the United States, in Scandinavia, Switzerland, and in the Canadian province of Alberta as late as the 1970s. And even today there are those in some parts of the world (notably the Balkans) who promote the idea of 'ethnic cleansing' in the name of national solidarity and racial purity.

Chapter 3

Eugenics and the Intellectuals

Introduction

The popularity of eugenic theories among many intellectuals and political thinkers in Britain in the early decades of the twentieth century must be seen against the background of some of the major issues which preoccupied people as the Victorian era (1837–1901) was drawing to a close.

The 1870s had triggered a long and heated debate about whether Britain had entered a period of economic decline. After decades of undisputed industrial supremacy, the country was experiencing falling prices, narrower profit margins and stiff competition from German and American manufacturers who clearly benefited from larger domestic markets and greater natural resources. 'The day of small nations has long passed away,' declared Joseph Chamberlain, the leading late-Victorian politician in a speech made in Birmingham in May 1904, 'the day of Empires has come' (quoted in Pugh, 2005, p. 11). Although Britain possessed an extensive and still-expanding empire, much of her overseas territory remained thinly populated and vulnerable to rival powers. Many imperialists argued that Britain was failing to exploit the economic potential of her imperial possessions. And beneath these growing concerns over industrial decline and the future of the empire lay a fundamental unease about the moral condition of British society during the last decades of the nineteenth century. Revelations by Charles Booth and Seebohm Rowntree in the late 1890s about the extent of urban poverty in Britain provoked anxieties about the spread of a physically degenerate population in the cities, which, in turn, raised further doubts about Britain's future as an imperial power. It was feared that if society encouraged the procreation of its 'least fit' members, this would exacerbate the process of industrial, military and imperial decline.

The nineteenth century had been a period of rapid population growth (see Briggs, 1959, p. 394; Read, 1979, pp. 6, 214), a situation which alarmed a number of novelists and poets who embraced eugenic theories. For example: H. G. Wells declared in his 1905 novel *Kipps* that 'the extravagant swarm of new births' was 'the essential disaster of the nineteenth century' (Wells, 1905a, p. 282). The population of England and Wales had, in fact, grown from just under nine million at the time of the first national census in 1801 to nearly 18 million in 1851, the year of the Great Exhibition. This expansion had continued in the second half of the century, decade by decade: to around 20 million in 1861, 22,700,000 in 1871, 26 million in 1881, 29 million in 1891 and 32,500,000 in 1901. The reports accompanying the publication of these census figures had invariably commented on the fact that during Queen Victoria's 'happy reign', millions of people had been added to the total of her subjects, at the same time emphasizing, as, for example, in the 1871 *Report*, that this had been achieved 'not by the seizure of neighbouring territories, but mainly by the enterprise, industry and virtue of her people' (quoted in Read, 1979, p. 6). The industry of the Victorians in matters of reproduction had certainly been impressive, with the period witnessing a rise in the birth rate – and a corresponding fall in the death rate – in most parts of the country and generally throughout society; but at the turn of the century, things were beginning to change.

Leading intellectuals and campaigners among Britain's eugenicists – and particularly H. G. Wells, Aldous Huxley and birth control pioneer Marie Stopes – were to express great concern about the changing *nature* of population growth in the early decades of the twentieth century, since this growth appeared to contemporaries to be largely restricted to members of the immigrant and working classes. In fact, there had recently been a steady decline in the birth rate among the middle classes, from 35 per thousand population in the 1870s to 24 per thousand in 1914 (see Pugh, 2005, p. 13). It seemed to be the less populous well-to-do, rather than the despised lower orders, who disliked the idea of large families and were practising birth control;[1] and in a situation already aggravated by the effects of war, there were fears that the social fabric was in danger of being torn apart by an overpopulated proletariat.

Those who shared these major concerns about overpopulation and the perceived threat to the social structure and health of the nation came together in 1907 to set up the Eugenics Education Society, with the declared aim of 'furthering eugenic teaching and understanding in the home, in the schools and elsewhere'. This Society (known simply as the Eugenics Society after 1926) soon enjoyed a degree of influence out of all proportion to the actual size of its membership, which was never at any stage particularly large. It could claim the support of a number of leading politicians, doctors and physicians; and it was very skilful at propagating its views. As we saw in Chapter 2, it organized the First International Congress of Eugenics which was held in London in July 1912. In the next section, we will be concentrating on the utopian visions of some of the novelists and poets who championed the Society's work.

Eugenic Utopias

While many twentieth-century writers were influenced by eugenic ideas of one kind or another – and certainly racist, and specifically anti-Semitic, elements can be detected in the work of such popular authors as Hilaire Belloc, John Buchan, G. K. Chesterton and Agatha Christie – this section of the chapter will focus on the work of H. G. Wells, D. H. Lawrence, T. S. Eliot, Aldous Huxley and W. B. Yeats.

It is interesting to note at the start of this section that the idea of sketching out a eugenic utopia had, in fact, occupied Francis Galton in the closing months of his life. The title of the work, which was never published, was *Kantsaywhere*; and, in Nicholas Gillham's view, 'it expressed more clearly than any dry scientific paper or popular article what Galton hoped eugenics would achieve' (Gillham, 2001, p. 343). All the inhabitants of Kantsaywhere were required to take an examination that vetted them genetically. Failures could not live in mainstream society, but were segregated in labour colonies where conditions were not particularly onerous but where strict celibacy was enforced. Those passing the examination with a 'second-class certificate' could propagate 'with reservations'. Those who did well could move on to take the honours examination at the Eugenics College of Kantsaywhere where successful students were granted 'diplomas for heritable gifts, physical and mental'. These elite individuals were allowed, indeed encouraged, to intermarry and have large numbers of children.

Where H. G. Wells was concerned, it has been suggested by Professor John Carey that it was 'anxiety about overpopulation', rooted in his childhood vision of the woods and fields destroyed at Bromley in Kent where he was born in 1866, that was the key both to 'his reading of modern history' and to 'his views as to what constituted the ideal society' (see Carey, 1992, p. 119). Yet Wells was not a one-dimensional thinker; and in the early years of the twentieth century, he struggled to reconcile his eugenic views with his support for the philosophy of the Fabian Society. This Society had been founded in 1884 as a kind of think-tank and talking shop for those left-wing middle-class intellectuals who argued for the gradual evolution of modern society towards socialism, but rejected the notion of class struggle and any prospect of violent revolution along Marxist lines. Wells was flattered to be elected as a member of this exclusive intellectual club in 1903, one of his sponsors being George Bernard Shaw. Since many of his non-fiction books and articles called for a radical transformation of British society by the application of rational planning and new technology, he seemed to be a natural recruit to the Fabians, but his abrasive manner soon antagonized existing members of the Society, and after a very short period, his active involvement with its affairs rapidly diminished and eventually ceased. Wells's 'socialist' philosophy, if indeed his thinking actually *deserves* that label, was essentially elitist and autocratic – and based on the idea that a select group of individuals understood which social policies were in the best interests of the working class and should be given free scope to implement them.

The 'threat' of overpopulation – a key cause of concern for all eugenicists of the period – figured in a number of Wells's works, both fiction and non-fiction. While for many well-informed contemporary commentators, steady population growth was an exciting and positive development, providing the impetus to increased productivity and social mobility, for Wells, it was a totally *malign* trend that had to be reversed – particularly since it seemed to be confined to unskilled immigrants and the urban working class. In *The World of William Clissold*, published in 1926, the hero observed that nineteenth-century gains in productivity had actually been 'absorbed by blind breeding' (quoted in Carey, 1992, p. 119). Support for birth control became for Clissold, as indeed for Wells himself, the vital test of a modern world view – the crucial factor distinguishing liberals from hopeless reactionaries. Indeed, Wells's implacable hostility to the Catholic Church arose from his perception that its opposition to all forms of birth control stood in the way of any improvement in the human condition.

Wells's eugenic solutions to the problems faced by modern society can be found chiefly in two of his major non-fiction works: *Anticipations* (full title *Anticipations of the Reaction of Mechanical and Scientific Progress Upon Human Life and Thought*), published

in 1901, and *A Modern Utopia*, published in 1905. In these influential texts, Wells committed himself to formulating ways in which
'inferior' breeds could be eliminated or at least prevented from
breeding and the threat of a world dominated by the illiterate
masses thereby averted. For Wells, 'representative democracy' was
a degenerate form of government, responsible for poor legislation
and terrible wars. It should be replaced by an authoritarian 'socialist'
government in the hands of an aristocracy of well-educated, scientifically minded men committed to halting the advance of the mass
of low-grade humanity currently monopolizing the world's
resources.

In *Anticipations*, Wells observed that 'gallstones of vicious,
helpless and pauper masses' had appeared all over the world,
representing an integral part of the processes of industrialization
and mechanical progress, 'as inevitable in the social body as are
waste matters and disintegrating cells in the body of an active and
healthy man' (Wells, 1901, pp. 46–7). He labelled these 'great
useless masses of people' the 'People of the Abyss', and he
predicted that the ideal state of his dreams would have to take
radical measures to avoid social catastrophe and attain a dominant
position in the world:

> The law that dominates the future is glaringly plain. A people
> must develop and consolidate its educated efficient classes or
> face social ruin and be beaten in war. . . . The war of the coming
> time will really be won in schools and colleges and universities,
> wherever men write and read and talk together. The nation
> that produces in the near future the largest proportional devel-
> opment of educated and intelligent engineers and agriculturists,
> of doctors, schoolmasters, professional soldiers and intellec-
> tually active people of all sorts and the nation that also most
> resolutely picks over, educates, sterilizes, exports or poisons its
> People of the Abyss . . . will certainly be the nation that will be
> the most powerful in warfare as in peace, and will certainly be
> the ascendant or dominant nation in the twentieth century.
> (ibid., p. 120)

In the last chapter of *Anticipations*, Wells outlined some of the
policies and attitudes that would characterize his ideal state, to be
known as the New Republic. Above all, there must be no conces-
sions to vague notions of equality or social justice:

It has become apparent that whole masses of human population are, as a whole, inferior in their claim upon the future to other masses, that they cannot be given opportunities or trusted with power as the superior peoples are trusted, that their characteristic weaknesses are contagious and detrimental in the civilizing fabric, and that their range of incapacity tempts and demoralizes the strong. To give them equality is to sink to their level; to protect and cherish them is to be swamped in their fecundity. (ibid., p. 163)

The 'ethical system' envisaged by Wells would involve favouring the procreation of all those who were deemed worthy specimens of humanity, both physically and mentally, and, at the same time, halting the procreation of those 'base and servile types' who were not fit to live in a civilized society. In some cases, men would have to be killed for the sake of the common good:

The ethical system of the men of the New Republic, the ethical system which will dominate the world-state, will be shaped primarily to favour the procreation of all that is fine and efficient and beautiful in humanity – beautiful and strong bodies, clear and powerful minds and a growing love of knowledge – and to check the procreation of base and servile types, of fear-driven and cowardly souls, of all that is mean and ugly and bestial in the souls, bodies or habits of men. . . . And the method that nature has followed hitherto in the shaping of the world, whereby weakness was prevented from propagating weakness, and cowardice and feebleness were saved from the accomplishment of their desires, the method that must in some cases still be called in to the help of man, is death. In this new vision, death is no inexplicable horror, no pointless terminal terror to the miseries of life; it is, in fact, the end of all the pain of life, the end of the bitterness of failure, the merciful obliteration of weak and silly and pointless things. (ibid., pp. 167–8)

Wells predicted that the men of the New Republic would not be squeamish in facing or inflicting death because they would hold life to be a privilege and a responsibility, 'not a sort of night refuge for base spirits out of the void'. All killing would be done with an opiate, for 'death is too grave a thing to be made painful or dreadful'. Every effort would be made to avoid unnecessary brutality and justify the action taken:

The constant infliction of pain *for the sake of the pain* is against the better nature of man, and it is unsafe and demoralizing for anyone to undertake this duty. To kill under the seemly conditions science will offer is a far less offensive thing. . . . People who cannot live happily and freely in the world without spoiling the lives of others are better out of it. That is a current sentiment even today, but the men of the New Republic will have the courage of their opinions. (ibid., pp. 169–70)

There remained the 'problems' posed by the Jews and by the 'primitive' and 'inferior' peoples of Africa and Asia. According to Wells in the final paragraph of *Anticipations*, 'there is something very ugly about many Jewish faces'; but he was then quick to point out that 'there are Gentile faces just as coarse and gross'. The Jew was 'mentally and physically precocious', and could not be said to pose a threat to civilized values. In any case, the increasing number of intermarriages of Jews and Gentiles would, in Wells's view, be sufficient to cause Jews to 'cease to be a physically distinct element in human affairs in a century or so' (ibid., p. 178).

It was impossible to be equally sanguine about the 'problem' of the black and brown races of the world. Here the only viable solution appeared to be genocide. The 'swarms of black and brown and dirty-white and yellow people' who did not 'meet the new needs of efficiency' would have to be wiped out. So far as they failed to develop 'sane, vigorous and distinctive personalities for the great world of the future', it was clearly their portion to die out and disappear (ibid. p. 178).

In *A Modern Utopia*, published in 1905, two hikers in the Swiss Alps, the narrator and a botanist, fell into a space-warp and suddenly found themselves in a parallel world, identical in geography to our own, but conducted on Wellsian principles. There was a single world government, English was the universal language and the rules of this utopian earth were enforced by an austere governing elite know as the 'Samurai'.

Once again, Wells was concerned with the treatment of society's 'degenerates' and 'inferior breeds':

It is our business to ask what Utopia will do with its congenital invalids, its idiots and madmen, its drunkards and men of vicious mind, its cruel and furtive souls, its stupid people, too stupid to be of use to the community, its lumpish, unteachable and unimaginative people? And what will it do with the man who is 'poor' all round, the rather spiritless, rather incompetent low-grade man, who on earth sits in the den of the sweater,[2] tramps the streets under the banner of the unemployed, or trembles – in another man's cast-off clothing, and with an infinity of hat-touching – on the verge of rural employment? . .. These people will have to be in the descendent phase, and the healthy species must be engaged in eliminating them; there is no escape from that, and, conversely, the people of exceptional quality must be ascendant. The better sort of people, so far as they can be distinguished, must have the fullest freedom of public service, and the fullest opportunity of parentage. And it must be open to every man to approve himself worthy of ascendency. (Wells, 1905b, pp. 95–6)

In May 1904, when he had already started working on *A Modern Utopia*, Wells had joined George Bernard Shaw in the audience for a lecture given by Francis Galton at the London School of Economics with the title 'Eugenics: its Definition, Scope and Aims'. This Lecture made a big impact on him, and while he could approve of much of its content, it seems that he began to have misgivings about some of the more extreme implications of Galton's philosophy. He had also been distressed by the hostile (indeed horrified) criticism of *Anticipations* from many reviewers and friends. And all this may help to explain why the specific eugenic proposals in the 1905 work represented something of a 'retreat' from the positions adopted in 1901.[3] As we see in the passage quoted above, Wells still talked about 'eliminating' adult degenerates and failures; but this was no longer to be achieved by killing, even though this was often Nature's remedy. There would be incarceration and sterilization, but 'no killing, no lethal chambers'. It might be necessary to kill all 'deformed and monstrous and evilly diseased births'; but inferior adults would simply be 'prevented from breeding' (ibid., p. 100).

Wells never lost his enthusiasm for a world state ruled by an elite of intelligent, science-trained leaders; and, in various works, he gave his rulers such names as the 'Samurai', 'New Ironsides', 'Cromwellians', 'Open Conspirators' and the 'Air Police'. For a while, he even viewed Lenin's 1917 Revolution in Russia as fulfilling his notion of a great state taken over by an efficient elite committed to governing society on rational lines. When he visited Russia and actually met Lenin – a visit he recorded in *Russia in the Shadows*, published in 1920 – he found fault with many aspects of Soviet-style communism, but there was *no* suggestion that he objected to its absence of democracy. There is no doubt that the world state depicted in *Anticipations* and in *A Modern Utopia* was a police state. Yet Wells never made it clear whether his ideal rulers would take power gradually or by means of a violent revolution. He was also vague as to how exactly all nations would come together to create a United States of the World, governed by a science-trained aristocracy that might eventually combine economic socialism with a weak form of representative democracy. Above all, he could never explain how his advocacy of eugenics as a sort of new religion was compatible with a socialist philosophy concerned with the welfare of all.

D. H. Lawrence's enthusiastic support for eugenic solutions to society's perceived 'problems' derived from his reading of the works of Friedrich Nietzsche, which he discovered in Croydon Public Library in 1908. Many eugenicists looked for inspiration to the works of Nietzsche and, in particular, to *Also Sprach Zarathustra*, which had been written between 1883 and 1885.[4] In the Prologue to Part One of this controversial work, Zarathustra came down out of solitude, announced that God was dead and welcomed his successor, 'the Superman'. Nietzsche believed that the great majority of men had no right to existence, but were simply 'a misfortune to higher beings'.

The idea that mass existence was distinctly mediocre and could not properly be called 'life' had a strong appeal for the young Lawrence who was also very happy to accept Nietzsche's idea that the breeding of a future 'master race' would necessarily entail the annihilation of millions of 'failures'.[5] In a remarkable passage in a letter written in 1908, he outlined to his friend Blanche Jennings how he would deal with 'society's outcasts':

If I had my way, I would build a lethal chamber as big as the Crystal Palace, with a military band playing softly, and a Cinematograph working brightly; then I'd go out into the back streets and main streets and bring them in, all the sick, the halt and the maimed; I would lead them gently, and they would smile me a weary thanks; and the band would softly bubble out 'the Hallelujah Chorus' (Boulton, 1979, p. 81, quoted in Carey, 1992, p. 12).

Lawrence believed passionately that in his ideal society the masses should be prevented from learning how to read and write. He also shared the view put forward in *Also Sprach Zarathustra* that the very concept of universal education was one to be deplored and discarded. Nietzsche had argued that education should remain a 'privilege' so that higher beings could dominate all forms of written culture:

> Another century of mass readership and spirit itself will stink. ... That everyone can learn to read will ruin in the long run not only writing, but thinking too. .... Once spirit was God, then it became man, and now it is even becoming the mob. (Nietzsche, 1883–85, translated by Hollingdale, 1961, p. 67)

For Lawrence, it was essential that all schools for the masses should be closed immediately. Without the demands imposed by formal education, the working class would be free to lead a purely physical life. If there had to be some forms of instruction, boys would be expected to attend craft workshops, girls would study domestic science, and it would also be compulsory for boys to learn 'primitive modes of fighting and gymnastics'.

Lawrence's racism, and, in particular, his anti-Semitism, can be detected in a number of his works. In his 1928 novel *Lady Chatterley's Lover*, for example, he described Sir Clifford Chatterley as possessing 'a cold spirit of vanity, that had no warm human contacts, and that was as corrupt as any low-born Jew in craving for prostitution to the bitch-goddess, Success' (Lawrence, 1961 edition, p. 74).

Lawrence's anti-Semitic views were certainly shared by the poet T. S. Eliot (1888–1965) who was a fervent supporter of the Eugenic Society's aims and aspirations. An emphasis on the importance of good breeding and a view of the Jew as coming from 'inferior stock' are both apparent in the following lines from the poem 'Gerontion':

> My house is a decayed house,
> And the Jew squats on the window sill, the owner,
> Spawned in some estaminet of Antwerp,
> Blistered in Brussels, patched and peeled in London.

And in the poem 'Burbank with a Baedeker: Bleistein with a Cigar', we find:

> On the Rialto once.
> The rats are underneath the piles.
> The Jew is underneath the lot.

Fear and loathing of the Jews was a prominent feature of much eugenic thinking in Britain in the first half of the twentieth century. A key text in this regard was Houston Stewart Chamberlain's *The Foundations of the Nineteenth Century*, published in 1899, which argued that the race was threatened by racial impurity or mixing, the worst agents of which were the Jews; as Chamberlain put it: 'a mongrel is frequently very clever, but never reliable; morally he is always a weed' (Chamberlain, 1899, p. 261, quoted in Pugh, 2005, p. 13). Debates in the early decades of the century about moral degeneracy, racial rejuvenation, national unity and the Jews make it clear that Britain played a leading role in laying the theoretical foundations for the European preoccupation with race theory in the inter-war period. Indeed, we learn from the first volume of Professor Ian Kershaw's recent Biography of Hitler that the Nazi Leader drew heavily on Chamberlain's anti-Semitic writing in developing his own polemic against the Jews (Kershaw, 1998, pp. 78, 135, 151). Some eugenicists in Britain were later to be appalled by revelations of the true nature of Hitler's campaign against the Jews; but they could not escape the blame for fostering a view of Jewish culture as representing a way of life fit only for extermination.

Returning to the theme of 'eugenic utopias', and moving on to the work of Aldous Huxley (1894–1963), it might at first seem that Huxley's *Brave New World* does not really belong in this section, since it has become, together with George Orwell's 1949 classic *Nineteen Eighty-Four*, one of the twin pillars of the *anti-utopian* tradition in English Literature and a 'byword' for all that is most repellent and 'nightmarish' in the world of the future. Yet it is not clear that Huxley himself viewed his vision of the world to come in quite that way.

First published in 1932, *Brave New World* was set in 'this year of stability, A. F. 632', and, by this, Huxley meant 632 years after the time of the American car magnate Henry Ford who had brought mass production to the car industry, flooding America with fifteen million Model 'T' Fords by 1927. Ford was the presiding deity of Huxley's model World State, a global caste system divided into ten zones, each run by a Resident World Controller. Through clever use of genetic engineering, brainwashing and recreational sex and drugs, all the inhabitants of this ideal society were happy consumers. Only in the various Savage Reservations, existing beyond the boundaries of the World State, was the old 'imperfect way of life' allowed to continue.

It has been argued that the composition of *Brave New World* proved really problematic for Huxley between April and August 1931 because he was unsure in his own mind whether he was writing a satire, a prophecy or a blueprint.[6] When a journalist asked him in 1935 whether his ultimate sympathies lay with 'the savages' aspirations or with the ideal of conditioned stability', Huxley is reported to have replied: 'With neither, but I believe some mean between the two is both desirable and possible, and must be our objective'. It is, of course, hugely significant that *Brave New World* was written at the time of the Great Depression in America and Europe. In the same way that H. G. Wells's *Anticipations* and *A Modern Utopia* were inspired less by a prospect of the distant future than by a morbid fear of overpopulation and the rule of the ignorant masses, which obsessed Wells at the beginning of the twentieth century, so the ideas in *Brave New World* were shaped by the economic crisis and political inertia which characterized the early 1930s. Huxley actually had a great deal in common with Wells in the 1920s and early 1930s, and they shared, in particular, a contempt for most forms of parliamentary democracy and a belief that a healthy society must be organized as a hierarchy of mental quality controlled by an elite caste of scientifically trained experts. In January 1932, shortly before the publication of *Brave New World*, Huxley gave a talk on BBC Radio in which he discussed the beneficial potential of eugenics as an instrument of political control, and expressed a readiness to sanction eugenic measures as a means of arresting 'the rapid deterioration of the whole West European stock'. Yet in his 1946 Foreword to *Brave New World*, Huxley made no reference to the appeal which eugenics had held for him in the early 1930s. The atrocities committed by Adolf Hitler and his Nazi associates had brought all eugenic theories into disrepute. Instead, the new Foreword emphasized that, unless we learned the lessons of the past, we had only two alternatives to choose from: 'either a number of national, militarised totalitarianisms, having as their root the terror of the atomic bomb and as their consequence the destruction of civilization (or, if the warfare is limited, the perpetuation of militarism); or else one *supra-national* totalitarianism, called into existence by the social chaos resulting from rapid technological progress in general and the atom revolution in particular' (Huxley, 1946 edition, p. 38).

Finally, in this section, we look at the later work of the poet W. B. Yeats (1865–1939), whose keen interest in eugenic theories was reinforced by his reading of Raymond B. Cattell's *The Fight for Our*

National Intelligence, published in 1937.[7] Both Cattell and Yeats were excited by the passing of the Eugenic Sterilization Law in Nazi Germany in 1933, already discussed in Chapter 2. Cattell congratulated Hitler's Government for being the first European administration to have the courage to promote compulsory sterilization of the unfit as a means of securing racial improvement; and Yeats praised the Nazis and other Fascist organizations for recognizing that European civilization had indeed reached a crisis.

A preoccupation with the importance of good breeding can be easily detected in the following lines from one of Yeats's last poems 'Under Ben Bulben',[8] composed in 1938:

> Irish poets, learn your trade,
> Sing whatever is well made,
> Scorn the sort now growing up
> All out of shape from toe to top,
> Their unremembering hearts and heads
> Base-born products of base beds.

But it was *On the Boiler*,[9] a piece of social commentary written in 1938 and published in 1939, the year of Yeats's death, that contained the poet's most forthright exposition of eugenic theories. It was here that Yeats referred to the conviction of a number of 'well-known specialists' that the principal European nations were all degenerating 'in body and in mind', though, in Yeats's view, the evidence for this had been suppressed *both* by most politicians in case it damaged their standing in their constituencies and by the popular newspapers in case it harmed circulation (Yeats, 1939b, republished in Larrissy, 1997, p. 391).

Yeats accepted Raymond Cattell's view that something termed 'innate intelligence' – or what Yeats called 'mother-wit' – could now be measured, especially in children, with great accuracy. If, for example, you took a pair of twins and educated one in wealth, the other in poverty, tests administered at various stages in their adult lives would show that 'their "mother-wit" would be the same'. Then again, if you picked a group of 'slum children' and moved them to a better neighbourhood with all the benefits of 'better food, light and air', it would have little or no effect on their 'intelligence'. It followed that all social welfare schemes and educational reforms were useless as 'improvers of the breed'. Yeats quoted with approval a saying popular with George Bernard Shaw to the effect that 'you couldn't make a silk purse out of a sow's ear' (ibid., pp. 391, 393).

It was obvious to Yeats, relying on some dubious statistics supplied by Cattell, that the lower orders were breeding at an astonishing rate, and that, sooner or later, ways would have to be found of limiting the families of the unintelligent classes.

> Since about 1900, the better stocks have not been replacing their numbers; while the stupider and less healthy have been more than replacing theirs. Unless there is a marked change in the public mind, every rank above the lowest must degenerate, and as inferior men push up into the gaps, society must degenerate more and more quickly. The results of promoting the stupid and the unhealthy are already visible in the degeneration of literature, newspapers and amusements (there was once a stock company playing Shakespeare in every considerable town); and, I am convinced, in benefactions like that of Lord Nuffield,[10] a self-made man, to Oxford, which must gradually substitute applied science for ancient wisdom. (ibid., p. 393)

As a way of tackling the problem of overpopulation, particularly of the unhealthy and feebleminded, Yeats went as far as to quote with approval what he believed to be an ancient custom in Scotland:

> If any were visited with the falling sickness, madness, gout, leprosy, or any of a whole range of dangerous diseases, which were likely to be propagated from the father to the son, he was instantly gelded; a woman would be kept from all company of men; and if, by chance, having some disease, she was found to be with child, she and her entire brood would have to be buried alive; and this would be done for the common good, less the whole nation should be injured or corrupted.

At this point in the commentary, Yeats urged his readers not to be too squeamish about this drastic but acceptable remedy:

> A severe doom, you will say, and *not* one to be used among Christians; yet worthy to be looked into more than it is. For now, by our too much facility in this matter, in giving way for all to marry that wish to and too much liberty and indulgence in tolerating all sorts, there is a vast confusion of hereditary diseases, no family secure, no man free from some grievous infirmity or other. . . . And so it comes to pass that our generation is corrupt, we have too many weak persons, both in body

and in mind, many feral diseases raging amongst us, crazed families . . . our fathers bad, and we are like to be worse. (ibid., pp. 390–1)

It was also of great concern to Yeats that the better organization of agriculture and industry was threatening to enable the lower classes to procure 'all the necessities of life' and thereby remove 'the last check upon the multiplication of the ineducable masses'. If this 'threat' ever became a reality, it would become 'the duty of the educated classes' to seize and control 'one or more of those necessities'. Yeats foresaw a prolonged civil war between the elite orders and 'the drilled and docile masses'. He pointed out with some satisfaction that during the Great War, Germany had had only 400 submarine commanders and that 60 per cent of the damage to allied shipping had been the work of just 24 men. Yet there was always the danger that the upper classes would not have the courage to fight. The most horrifying thought of all was that the European civilization – 'like those older civilizations that saw the triumph of their gangrel stocks' – would simply accept decay. In Yeats's view, recalling sentiments first expressed in his earlier work 'A Vision', published in 1925, 'we must love war because of its horror, so that belief many be changed and civilization renewed' (ibid., p. 394).

The Campaign for Birth Control and Voluntary Sterilization

Marie Stopes's *Married Love* (Stopes, 1918) was published in March 1918 and immediately became the subject of much controversy. While it could be seen simply as a plea for marital sexual harmony, it also urged men and women to enjoy sex and use artificial forms of contraception. Many called the book a blatant charter for prostitution; and, for many years, it was banned in America as 'obscene'.

We have already seen that it was a major concern of eugenicists that it seemed to be the upper and middle classes, rather than the fertile lower orders, who were regularly practising birth control in the early decades of the century; and Marie Stopes shared this concern. She had become a eugenicist at the age of 32 in 1912, and this had pre-dated her interest in the birth control issue. (The first birth-control clinic in Britain was actually established in 1921.) It was Marie Stopes's view in the 1920s that 'the flower of English manhood' had been killed in the First World War, before having the opportunity to produce hordes of children with 'suitable character-istics'. She agreed with the prominent Fabian Society thinker Sidney Webb in believing that too many children were being born to various classes of immigrants such as Irish Roman Catholics and Polish, Russian and German Jews, along with casual labourers, the thriftless poor and the feeble-minded – a trend which must result in national deterioration. She often took things to quite extraordinary extremes, having a marked distaste for all forms of physical defect and virtually cutting off relations with her only child when he married a *bespec-tacled* woman; she called the marriage 'a eugenic crime'.[11]

Marie Stopes's work certainly angered the Roman Catholic Church which, in addition to finding all eugenic principles unacceptable, also opposed the use of all forms of artificial birth control. In 1922, Stopes found herself in real conflict with T. P. O'Connor, the Catholic President of the British Board of Film Censors (BBFC) when she produced a screen version of her 1918 best seller (see Matthews, 1994, p. 37). Although the screenplay actually bore little relationship to the sophisticated themes of *Married Love*, being a romantic drama focusing on the relationship between a South London parlourmaid and her fireman boyfriend, it did make the point that marriage need not necessarily lead to the creation of oversized families, and this caused great offence to O'Connor who argued for a complete ban. He was, however, opposed by the London County Council (LCC), and, after months of protracted discussion, Stopes won a significant victory when the film was finally released with a few minor cuts.

One of the major campaigns in which eugenicists played a prominent part in the 1920s and 1930s was that for voluntary sterilization of the feebleminded. As we shall see, it was the lobbying of eugenicists which led, in 1932, to the appointment by the Minister of Health of a special committee – the Brock Committee – to report and make recommendations on the voluntary or compulsory steril-ization of the feebleminded in England and Wales. The Committee was intended to generate support for a Royal Commission on the question, an inquiry which would then, in turn, provide the basis for new legislation. In the words of Professor Desmond King who has made a special study of the subject, 'this was potentially the most substantial policy achievement of the eugenics movement in Britain' (King, 1999, p. 64). In this section we will examine the context of the Brock Committee's appointment, a context in which eugenic arguments commanded considerable support among the political and intellectual elite in this country.

The organizational focus of the campaign for voluntary sterilization was the Eugenics Education Society, which, as we saw earlier in the chapter, had been founded in 1907. Similar campaigns were led in their respective countries by the German Society for Racial Hygiene, founded in Berlin in 1905, the Eugenics Record Office established in the US in 1910 and the French Eugenics Society founded in Paris in 1912. To begin with, sterilization was just one of *four* strategies embraced by leading eugenicists in Britain for dealing with the problem of the feebleminded, the others being marital regulation, birth control and segregation. There ensued a long-running debate within the Eugenics Society as to whether 'mental defectives' should be segregated or sterilized – a debate that was eventually won by the proponents of sterilization, this also then being the course of action that the Brock Committee was expected to recommend in the 1930s.

The strong influence of the eugenics movement on political debate is indicated by the 1909 decision of Winston Churchill, at that time President of the Board of Trade, to circulate, as a Cabinet paper, a speech by the leading eugenicist Alfred Tredgold on the (related) subjects of poverty and feeblemindedness. Then, shortly after becoming Home Secretary in February 1910, Churchill wrote a letter to Prime Minister Herbert Asquith articulating his fear of the high birth rate among the feebleminded:

I am convinced that the multiplication of the Feebleminded, which is proceeding now at an artificial rate, unchecked by any of the old constraints of nature and actually fostered by new civilized conditions, is a very terrible danger to the race. The number of children in feebleminded families is calculated at 7.4; whereas in normal families, it is but 4.2. . . . There are 12,000 feebleminded and defective children in our Special Schools; many others are in residential homes. . . . The girls come out by the thousand at 16, are the mothers of imbeciles at 17 and thereafter, with surprising regularity, they frequent our workhouse lying-in wards year by year. The males contribute an ever-broadening streak to the insane or half-insane crime which darkens the life of our towns and fills the convict prisons. (Letter from Churchill to Asquith, December 1910, quoted in King, 1999, p. 69)

The first major success of the eugenic lobbyists came with the passage of the Mental Deficiency Act in 1913, based on the recommendations of the Royal Commission on the Care and Control of the Feebleminded which met between 1904 and 1908 and issued its Report in 1908. The Act specified four categories of individuals who were liable to detention in mental institutions: idiots, imbeciles, the feebleminded and moral imbeciles. Until the passage of this Act, the term 'feebleminded' had remained vague and conceptually confused. Now the feebleminded were defined as: 'persons in whose case there exists from birth or from early age mental defectiveness not amounting to imbecility, yet so pronounced that they require care, supervision and control for their own protection or for the protection of others, or, in the case of children, that they by reason of such defectiveness, appear to be permanently incapable of receiving proper benefit from the instruction in ordinary schools' (quoted in King, 1999, p. 70).

Eugenicists expected great things from the Brock Committee set up in 1932. Sir Lawrence Brock, who gave his name to the Committee, had close contacts with eugenic activists, and two of its key members, Alfred Tredgold and Ronald Fisher, were prominent members of the Eugenics Society. It held 36 meetings, took evidence from 60 expert witnesses and received a large amount of statistical data. In the course of its proceedings, members rejected the idea of *compulsory* sterilization, but decided that, for those 'mental defectives' likely to return to the community, there was a strong argument for establishing the opportunity to consent to *voluntary* sterilization. This was, in fact, the course of action recommended by the Committee when it finally reported in 1934; but a Royal Commission was never to be appointed, and there was to be no government enthusiasm for legislative enactment as the findings of the Committee were discreetly laid to one side.

Professor King has suggested four main reasons to account for the ultimate failure of the long campaign to introduce voluntary sterilization. In the first place, there was the opposition of the Minister of Health, Sir E. Hilton Young, and of other members of Ramsay MacDonald's National Government. Politicians' opposition reflected a concern that the whole issue was little understood by the public. Many failed to understand the distinction between sterilization and castration; and it was popularly believed that the promotion of sterilization was simply part of a cynical campaign to reduce the spending on institutions for those with learning disabilities. Secondly, there was the bitter opposition of the Labour Movement and of the Catholic Church. Most trade unionists believed the whole idea of sterilization to be anti-working class; and

Catholics argued that it violated a God-given right to reproduce. Although Catholics made up only six per cent of the population, they constituted a group whom ministers did not wish to offend. Thirdly, although the Brock Report cited a strong scientific case for sterilization, an absence of sufficient confidence in the evidence weakened the eugenicists' case. The British Medical Association refused to endorse voluntary sterilization; and eugenicists themselves were unable to agree on the number of mental defectives whose condition clearly resulted from hereditary factors. Finally, the Nazi sterilization programme (already discussed in Chapter 2) irreparably discredited its proposed British counterpart. The German Law, operative from the beginning of 1934, quickly became associated with all manner of cruel medical practices; and it seemed to be only a small group of misguided zealots who admired the policies that the German Government was pursuing.[12]

Chapter 4

IQ and Eleven-Plus Selection

Introduction

We have already seen that eugenic theories exerted a powerful influence on the thinking of a number of prominent novelists and poets in Britain in the first half of the twentieth century, and that such ideas underpinned campaigns, in Britain and elsewhere, to identify and deal with those who might undermine the racial stock of the nation. But it was in the area of intelligence testing that Galton's views on heredity and class were to make their most lasting impact.

Galton was not, of course, alone in believing that intelligence and ability were largely inherited characteristics which could be measured with a fair degree of accuracy. While his eugenic creed was steadily gaining in popularity and respectability in Britain at the turn of the century, educational psychology in a number of countries was increasingly preoccupied with the development of the pseudo-science of 'psychometry' – the precise measurement and testing of mental ability states and processes. In France in 1904, the Ministry of Public Instruction entrusted Alfred Binet (1857–1911) with the task of devising tests for Parisian schoolchildren designed initially to distinguish between those pupils who were 'mentally retarded' and those who were 'performing badly' for a variety of other reasons. Binet's first tests were published in 1905, and before Galton died, these had been improved, first in 1908 and again in 1911. And as these early tests were refined, so their scope and usefulness apparently broadened: they could identify not only the 'mentally retarded', but also the 'above average' and the 'very bright'.

Other psychologists on both sides of the Atlantic joined in this kind of research, and in 1916, the Stanford-Binet test was devised, this being a revised version of the Binet test designed for American children and purporting to be able to predict future levels of ability on the basis of current scores. It was at this time that the concept of Intelligence Quotient came to the fore, in essence an expression of the relationship between 'ability' and chronological age translated into a convenient number by means of the beguilingly simple formula: IQ equals Mental Age divided by Chronological Age multiplied by 100. According to this formula, an IQ of 100 was, by definition, the norm or average score, and marks above or below 100 indicated the possession of 'above' or 'below' average intelligence. These tests were used during the First World War for selecting key personnel and allocating individual recruits to suitable jobs. In England, it was Galton's disciple Cyril Burt (1883–1971) who did more than anyone to advocate the widespread use of IQ tests for the purpose of pinning permanent labels on schoolchildren at the age of eleven.

The Career and Influence of Cyril Burt

The period from 1907 to the early 1930s has been described by Cyril Burt's biographer Leslie Hearnshaw as 'the heyday of Eugenics' (Hearnshaw, 1979, p. 48). As we have already seen, the Eugenics Education Society had been set up in 1907, with the aim of 'furthering eugenic teaching and understanding at home, in the schools and elsewhere' (see Chapters 2 and 3). The Society quickly became a very influential pressure group, and recruited a considerable proportion of its membership from leading scientists, university teachers and doctors concerned with preserving the 'virility' of the Anglo-Saxon 'race'. Although the impression is sometimes given that the Society was at its strongest in the years *before* the First World War, in simple numerical terms this is not the case. It was in the 1920s that the Society enjoyed an appreciable increase in numbers, culminating with the highest recorded annual membership of 768 in 1932 (see Brown, 1988, p. 300). It was of considerable benefit to the Society's prestige and respectability that in his will, Francis Galton bequeathed £45,000 to University College, London to establish a chair of eugenics. Galton's close friend and disciple Karl Pearson, who had been Professor of Applied Mathematics in the College since 1884, transferred to the new Chair in 1911, and held it until his retirement in 1933 (see Harte and North, 1978, p. 129; Wooldridge, 1994, p. 78).[1]

If we now concentrate on the process by which the eugenic theories put forward by Francis Galton and his disciples exerted a powerful influence on concepts of 'ability' and 'intelligence', with profound implications for social planning, it is important to look in detail at the life and career of Cyril Burt who worked tirelessly to ensure that his views on the nature of intelligence were translated into government policy and legislation. Finding means of classifying young children so that they followed the eugenically appropriate course for them was to be Burt's lifetime's work. Educational selection was to be one facet of that 'careful selection' highlighted by Burt's great mentor Galton in his account of the importance of planned breeding in the opening paragraph of *Hereditary Genius* (discussed in Chapter 2).

Born in March 1883, Cyril Burt spent most of his early life in the village of Snitterfield, some five miles from Stratford-upon-Avon, where his father worked as a conscientious family doctor. Dr Burt numbered members of the Galton family, who lived nearby at an estate in Claverdon, among his neighbours, friends and patients; and he was a particular admirer of Francis Galton who regularly came to stay there with his relatives. It was while accompanying his father on his rounds that the young Cyril Burt came into contact with Francis Galton, then in his seventies – a contact that was to be the major influence in shaping his career.

Cyril Burt later recalled the remarkable impression that Francis Galton had made upon his father:

> When my father had visited one of his more eminent patients, he would often try to fire my ambition by describing their achievements or those of their relatives. . . . Darwin Galton, an ailing old man of eighty, lived three miles away at Claverdon, where Sir Francis Galton now lies buried. And since, as family physician, my father used to call there at least once a week, I heard more about Francis Galton than about anyone else. Next to John Milton and Charles Darwin, he was, I think, my father's supreme example of the Ideal Man; and as a model, he had the further merit of being really alive. So it was that, on returning to school, I got from the Library Galton's *Inquiries into Human Faculty*, and I still recollect the superstitious thrill when I noticed on the title page that it first saw daylight in the same year (1883) that I was born. (Burt, 1952, pp. 58–9, quoted in White, 2006, p. 11)

The young Burt was equally awestruck by the elderly Galton, describing him later as 'one of the most distinguished-looking people I have ever known – tall, slim, neatly dressed, with a prominent forehead like the dome of St Paul's' (quoted in Norton, 1981, p. 305).

Having spent seven years as a pupil at Christ's Hospital in the City of London (1895 to 1902), with holidays invariably spent assisting his father in Snitterfield, Cyril Burt gained a scholarship to study classics at Jesus College, Oxford, and this was how he spent his undergraduate years, despite a strong wish to switch to science in preparation for a medical career. On leaving university, Burt decided to specialize in psychology; and it was in 1909, during a five-year period as Lecturer in Experimental Psychology at the University of Liverpool, that he wrote his career-establishing paper for the *British Journal of Psychology* entitled 'Experimental tests of general intelligence' (Burt, 1909). The conclusion he reached was that intelligence was inherited 'to a degree which few psychologists have hitherto legitimately ventured to maintain' (p. 177).

It was largely on the strength of this 1909 paper, which enjoyed a very positive reception, that Burt was appointed three years later to the position of official educational psychologist to the London County Council (LCC), a post which he was to hold from 1913 until his transfer to University College, London, as Professor of Psychology in 1932.[2] This LCC post gave Burt unprecedented power and influence, for, by the terms of the 1902 Education Act, local education authorities had responsibility for a wide range of educational and social activities covering a broad spectrum of the community.

From now on, in the words of Adrian Wooldridge (1994, p. 77), 'Burt devoted his life to refining Galton's intellectual legacy'. He revered Galton as 'the father of British psychology', arguing that he had made the first attempt to turn the study of individuals into a reputable branch of science and that he had established psychology as a *biological* science. Galton provided Burt with most of his ruling intellectual passions, notably a belief in the need to substitute a scientific procedure for casual observation and subjective impression; a keen interest in measurement and quantification; and an anxiety to prevent the deterioration of the race by ensuring that the 'able' and the 'gifted' were given the positions of authority in society that their intelligence merited.

The Galtonian conception of mental ability which Burt embraced contained the notion of innately determined limits, differing from one individual to another and parallel to those in human bodily development, of which Galton had made a special study. Burt also followed Galton's line of thinking in two other key respects. For both men, intelligence was in the broad sense of the term, an *intellectual* quality – that is to say, it characterized the *cognitive* rather than the *affective* or *conative* aspects of conscious behaviour. The enormous and measurable difference between the intellectual capacity of men [*sic*] was a theme running through every chapter of Galton's 1869 book *Hereditary Genius*. And for both men, intelligence, or natural innate ability, was also *general*. An individual might have a *specific* ability in mathematics or some other area of knowledge, but always underlying this was something more important and more all-encompassing. Galton believed that people generally laid too much emphasis on apparent specialities, believing, wrongly, that, because a man was devoted to some particular pursuit, he could not possibly have succeeded in anything else. And, as Professor John White has pointed out, a favourite saying of Burt's was that without a *special* gift for mathematics, a man could obviously not be a mathematician; but, at the same time, without a high degree of *general* ability, he could never be a *great* mathematician (White, 2006, p. 13).

We have noted that Burt took over from Galton a concern for measurement and precision; but it can, of course, be argued that at various stages in his career, he allowed his unshakeable belief in innate ability or intelligence to influence the way he interpreted and presented his data. As his biographer Professor Leslie Hearnshaw has written:

> Burt's belief in the innateness of intelligence was for him almost an article of faith, which he was prepared to defend against all opposition, rather than a tentative hypothesis to be refuted, if possible, by empirical tests. It is hard not to feel that, almost from the first, Burt showed an excessive assurance in the finality and correctness of his conclusions. The evidence for the innateness of intelligence he regarded at a very early stage as 'conclusive'. In the early 1920s he said, 'It is my personal conviction that the main outlines of our human nature are now approximately known, and that the whole territory of individual psychology has, by one worker or another, been completely covered in the main'. By the end of the 1940s, he was able to claim that all the more important group factors of ability had been identified. (Hearnshaw, 1979, p. 49)

Professor Hearnshaw's sentiments have been echoed by Stephen Jay Gould in his classic 1981 study *The Mismeasure of Man*, where he argued that Burt's zealous pursuit of his *idée fixe* acted as 'a distorter of judgment and finally as an incitement to fraud' (Gould, 1981, p. 274).

It was while working for the London County Council after 1913, where he was engaged in routine clinical work, particularly with the 'subnormal' and the 'delinquent', that Burt began to actively concern himself with the measurement of 'intelligence' and with the need to maintain the vigour of the Anglo-Saxon race. As was the case with others working in the field of child psychology at the start of the twentieth century, it was a eugenic concern with the problem of mental deficiency – often, as we have seen, referred to as 'feeble-mindedness' – that caused Burt to take a keen interest in the whole issue of intelligence testing. In an article for Volume 4 of *The Eugenics Review*, published in 1913, he emphasized that his growing interest in the data to be obtained from intelligence testing and his belief in the concept of 'mental inheritance' did indeed derive from his early concern with the problem of mental defectiveness, making particular reference to the findings of the 1908 Report on *The Care and Control of the Feebleminded* (Royal Commission, 1908):

> Of all cases of mental inheritance, the most fully established and most generally recognized is the inheritance of 'feeblemind-edness'. Feeblemindedness commonly dates from birth. Reference to the mental state of the parents and grandparents often discovers defects transmitted through three, four or even five generations. Perhaps the most convincing mass of evidence is that incidentally accumulated by the Royal Commission appointed at the commencement of this century to enquire into the quality of the provision made for the feebleminded. The majority of the witnesses called before it attached supreme importance in the causation of mental defect in children to a history of mental defect in the parents or near relatives; and the general opinion was that, 'apart from very rare accidental injuries, there is no such thing as manufactured feeblemind-edness'. (Burt, 1913, p. 172)

Burt was convinced of the profound significance of his basic proposition:

> However much we *try* to educate the ignorant, train the imbecile, cure the lunatic and reform the criminal, their offspring

will inherit, not the results of such education, but the original
ignorance; not the acquired training, but the original imbecility;
not the acquired sanity, but the original predisposition to lunacy;
not the moral reform, but the original tendency to crime. All our
work will have to be done afresh with each generation. (ibid.,
p. 184)

Moving on from a discussion of the twin problems of mental degeneracy and national deterioration, Burt's 1913 article made much
reference to the pioneering work of his mentor Francis Galton and
to the statistical evidence for the fact of 'mental inheritance' provided
by Karl Pearson in articles written for the journal *Bismetrika*, which
had been founded by Galton and Pearson in 1901. It was now
possible to state that 'the fact of mental inheritance . . . can no longer
be contested and its importance scarcely overestimated' (ibid., p.
183). In Burt's view, 'heredity remains indispensable to explain the
differences in mental capacities'. It was clearly essential to identify
those children who were simply not capable, by reason of mental
defect or feeblemindedness, of 'benefiting from the instruction given
in an ordinary elementary school' (ibid., p. 199).

Burt's article concluded with reflections on the racial implications of recent 'highly respected' anthropological studies:

It is important to recognize the presence of hereditary mental
differences even among the races of civilized Europe. Like the
differences between *civilized* and *uncivilized*, these differences
may be small. But even a slight bias may produce large
deflection. . . . These differences may well have sufficed, in the
national selection from those mental contents which form the
common stock of civilization, to determine a choice of institutions, customs and beliefs congenial rather than uncongenial to
the native temperament of each community or country. . . .
Mental inheritance, then, not only moulds the character of
individuals; it also rules the destiny of nations. . . . We must
conclude that there assuredly could be no problem upon which
historian and geographer, traveller and administrator, biologist
and experimentalist, statistician and psychologist could so fruit-
fully concentrate their wisdom as the problem of heredity and
its influence upon the mind. (ibid., pp. 199–200)

In the years following the First World War, many eugenicists urged
the value of intelligence testing upon the Board of Education. Most

notable among them was George Adami, the Vice-Chancellor of the University of Liverpool and author of *Medical Contributions to the Study of Evolution*, published in 1923. In an address to the International Eugenics Congress held in New York in September 1921 and reprinted in *The Eugenics Review* in 1923, Professor Adami emphasized the importance of turning from the problem of racial deterioration to that of selecting the best pupils for entry to the best schools, as preparation for occupying the leading positions in society. The major issue, he argued, was to find 'the real aristocracy of the nation'. He accepted that 'the social conditions of the present day are such as to favour the preponderance of what are from every point of view the lower classes, the survival of the unfit and the inevitable deterioration of the race' (Adami, 1923, p. 176); and yet, it would be wrong, in his view, for eugenicists to concentrate solely upon issues of national degeneracy. The need was to think positively and promote the propagation and wellbeing of the very best in the race:

> What I would urge is that here at last we have before us the obvious line of practical work for Eugenic Societies and the Eugenic Movement in general. Encourage the best! Either organize, or make the State organize, in every district a trained staff provided with a well-equipped set of rooms for the routine testing of every young person, whether male or female, when young, and then when he or she has reached the age of eighteen years. I say eighteen because while intelligence does not, so far as we can see, improve beyond the standard which some are capable of reaching at the age of sixteen, undoubtedly there are slow developers whose intellectual capacity, below normal at this life period, improves after the age of sixteen, while, in general, physical capacity is at its best at the age of eighteen, and, from other practical considerations, this latter age is the best for purposes of record. . . . We want to pick out the best in the community. And then having picked them out, publish their existence in the world. Establish an annual record of all the A1 youths and maidens of the year. . . . Think of the effect of such a publication. Think of the start in the world it would give to a man or a woman to be able to refer to his or her record as belonging to the A1 class, think of the status it would give him or her for the years to come, of the preferential treatment that would be afforded when applying for posts. Consider the preference the A1 man . . . would have in marriage, how parents

before giving their consent would require that he who sought their daughter's hand should produce his Eugenic Society Certificate and show where he stood in physical and mental capacity; of the advantage the A1 man would have in seeking the hand of a desirable damsel. Think how in years to come these annual publications would establish the good strains, a list of all the desirable families with which to become associated; how, in short, they would become the human stud book. (Adami, 1923, p. 185)[3]

Cyril Burt was certainly also of the opinion that the measurement of 'intelligence' should be used to pick out 'the best in the community'. His classic definition of 'human intelligence', which he believed could be measured with 'accuracy and ease', was clearly stated in a book for popular consumption called *How the Mind Works*, which was based on broadcast talks by a number of 'experts' on the new 'science' of mental testing given in 1933. In his own contribution to the symposium Burt argued that:

By the term 'intelligence', the psychologist understands *inborn, all-round intellectual ability*. It is inherited, or at least innate, not due to teaching or training; it is intellectual, not emotional or moral, and remains uninfluenced by industry or zeal; it is general, not specific, that is to say it is not limited to any particular kind of work, but enters into all we do or say or think. Of all our mental qualities, it is the most far-reaching; fortunately, it can be measured with accuracy and ease. (Burt, 1933, pp. 28–9)

As Professor Brian Simon, one of Burt's foremost critics from the 1950s onwards, observed in a book published in 1974: 'Here was a simple, clear, straightforward statement about the precise functioning of the human mind, admitting no doubts, inviting no argument' (Simon, 1974, p. 241).

Burt's views on the nature of intelligence and on the need for its accurate measurement exerted a powerful influence on government education policy in the 1920s and 1930s. As Leslie Hearnshaw has argued:

Outside psychology, it was . . . above all in the field of education that Burt was really influential. Between the two World Wars, his views and his findings impressed themselves on the leading policy-makers, particularly on the members of the Board of Education Consultative Committee, under the chairmanship, first of Sir Henry Hadow, and then of Mr (later Sir) Will Spens, whose Reports largely shaped the post-war reconstruction of the education system of England and Wales. (Hearnshaw, 1979, p. 111)

In the 1931 Hadow Report on *The Primary School*, Burt was responsible for the Appendix on the mental development of children between the ages of seven and eleven, which actually constituted the basis of the Committee's own observations. In the Spens Report on *Secondary Education*, published in 1938, Burt's influence was equally if not even more obvious. He provided a detailed memorandum on the mental development of children from the ages of eleven to sixteen, and argued strongly for the concept of innate general intelligence.

The Spens Report clearly played a major role in preparing the ground for the tripartite scheme of grammar, technical and secondary modern schools resulting from the popular interpretations of the 1944 Education Act, together with the selection procedure at eleven-plus. Its conclusions were expressed with great clarity and left little room for doubt:

Intellectual development during childhood appears to progress as if it were governed by a single central factor, usually known as 'general intelligence', which may be broadly described as innate all-round intellectual ability. It appears to enter everything which the child attempts to think, or say, or do, and seems on the whole to be the most important factor in determining his work in the classroom. Our psychological witnesses assured us that it can be measured approximately by means of adminis-tering intelligence tests. . . . Psychologists are confident that there are, in fact, wide individual differences in the development of general intelligence. For instance, there is strong evidence to show that the abler child continues to develop, though at a comparatively slow pace after puberty, till later than the average child. The less able child, and still more the mentally deficient child, comes earlier to a final stage in the development of general intelligence. We were informed that, with few exceptions, it is possible at a very early age to predict with some degree of accuracy the ultimate level of a child's intellectual powers; but this is true only of *general* intelligence, and does not necessarily hold good in respect of *specific* aptitudes or interests. The average child is said to attain the effective limit of development in general intelligence between the ages of sixteen and eighteen. Our psychological witnesses explained that this statement, which is sometimes misunderstood, does not imply that older boys and girls stop learning or that their *acquired* attainments, as distinct from their *innate* capacity, do not continue to increase. The child's *general* intelligence, which has been increasing up to the age of about sixteen to eighteen has, in the view of modern psychologists, then practically attained its maximum. (Board of Education, 1938, pp. 123–5)

The Spens Report explicitly considered, and rejected, the idea of 'multilateral' or 'comprehensive' schools and clearly held that all children should be allocated at the age of eleven to one or other of three types of secondary school according to their general ability and as preparation for a fulfilling and successful career in adult life. In a BBC Radio Third Programme talk broadcast in November 1950, Burt picked up this theme and argued that:

Obviously, in an ideal community, our aim should be to discover what ration of intelligence nature has given to each individual child at birth, then to provide him [*sic*] with the appropriate education, and finally to guide him into the career for which he seems to have been marked out. (reprinted in *The Listener*, 16 November 1950)

As far as Burt was concerned, recognition of this proposition meant upholding the values of a tripartite system of secondary schools with all children being educated in grammar, technical or secondary modern schools on the basis of their performance in the eleven-plus examination.

It has been argued by Adrian Wooldridge that 'Cyril Burt and his colleagues who dominated educational and psychological thinking in the 1920s and 1930s were actually meritocrats rather than conservatives and progressives rather than traditionalists'. According to this view, 'these psychologists combined a passion for measurement with a commitment to child-centred education'. Despite the arguments of their many detractors, 'their work was inspired by a desire to open admission to established institutions to "able children", regardless of their social origins, and to base education on the natural process of child development. In theory, their arguments were subversive of the social hierarchy; and, in practice, they provided important opportunities for able, working-class children to rise into the élite' (Wooldridge, 1994, pp. 16–17). Yet this view, by a leading Burt apologist, would seem to be contradicted by the fact that the psychologist followed his mentor Francis Galton in believing firmly that genius, high ability and advanced intelligence were largely confined to members of the upper and middle classes. Certainly the rigid selective education system based on intelligence testing that emerged in the 1940s and 1950s largely served to reinforce the assumptions underpinning the existing social structure; and it is this issue to which we will now turn in the next section.

The Divided Post-War Secondary System

Shortly after the Spens Report was published in 1938 the Second World War broke out, and no immediate steps were taken to implement its recommendations. Surprisingly early in the War, however, and well before final victory was in sight, members of the Coalition Government turned their attention to problems of post-war reconstruction. The Beveridge Report on Social Insurance appeared in 1942; and a year before this, in 1941, the newly-appointed President of the Board of Education, R. A. (Rab) Butler, set up a committee chaired by Dr Cyril Norwood, ex-Headmaster of Harrow School, to consider the curriculum and examinations to be used in state secondary schools. This Committee published its Report in 1943 (SSEC, 1943), almost simultaneously with the publication of the Board of Education's own White Paper on *Educational Reconstruction*, and together these key documents formed the basis of much of the 1944 Butler Education Act.

The Norwood Committee actually covered much the same ground as that dealt with by Spens and came broadly to the same conclusions. But, as many commentators have noted, its Report was much less scholarly and much more dogmatic. No evidence was taken from Cyril Burt or from any of his colleagues, and the findings of psychologists were largely ignored. The Committee was dominated by 'traditionalists' who had little or no sympathy with a theory of education which argued that its aims could be dictated by the provisional findings of particular sciences. Education had to be ultimately concerned with core values which were independent of time or a specific environment. *Experience*, not *psychology*, was sufficient to show that children obviously fell into three broad groups – the academic type, the technical type and the practical type – and that there must be three types of curriculum and three types of school to cater for all of them.

When the Norwood Committee was sitting, Cyril Burt was not living in London. He had moved with a large part of the staff of University College to Aberystwyth. As Leslie Hearnshaw has pointed out (1979, p. 117), 'it is doubtful if, even had he [Burt] been readily available, he would have been consulted'. The Committee, consisting wholly of educationists and educational administrators, called on evidence from teachers, commercial organizations and professional bodies, but did not see any reason to consult psychologists or social scientists. Not surprisingly, Burt was critical of the Report's findings and voiced his objections immediately in *The British Journal of Educational Psychology* (Burt, 1943). He even seemed to change his mind on matters with which he had previously been in agreement, expressing doubts, for example, on the desirability of eleven as the age of transition from primary to secondary school in England and Wales. It is, of course, hard not to suspect that a good deal of this criticism was actuated by pique at the virtual neglect of psychological evidence, including his own, and that this masked a fundamental agreement with the basic recommendations of the Report which, in principle, did not differ very much from those of the Spens Committee of which he had earlier approved.

As we have seen above, the Norwood Report itself argued that there should be three types of state secondary school catering for the three 'rough groupings' of children with correspondingly three different 'types of mind'. For each of these three groupings, a clearly defined type of curriculum was needed with its own particular bias:

> In a wise economy of secondary education, pupils of a particular type of mind would receive the training best suited for them and that training would lead them to an occupation where their capacities would be suitably used; that a future occupation is already present to their minds while they are still at school has been suggested, though, admittedly, the degree to which it is present varies. Thus, to the three main types of mind . . . there would correspond three main types of curriculum, which we may now attempt to indicate.

> First, there would be a curriculum of which the most characteristic feature is that it treats the various fields of knowledge as

suitable for coherent and systematic study for their own sake apart from immediate considerations of occupation, though, at a later stage, grasp of the matter and experience of the methods belonging to those fields may determine the area of choice of employment and may then contribute to success in the employment chosen.

The second type of curriculum would be closely, though not wholly, directed to the special data and skills associated with a particular kind of occupation; its outlook and its methods would always be bounded by a near horizon clearly envisaged. It would thus be closely related to industry, trades and commerce in all their diversity.

In the third type of curriculum, a balanced training of mind and body and a correlated approach to humanities, natural science and the arts would provide an equipment varied enough to enable pupils to take up the work of life: its purpose would not be to prepare for a particular job or profession, and its treatment would make a direct appeal to interests which it would awaken by a practical touch with affairs.

Of the first, it may be said that it may or may not look forward to university work; if it does, that is because the universities are traditionally concerned with the pursuit of knowledge as such. Of the second, we should say that it may or may not look forward to the universities, but that it should increasingly be directed to advanced studies in so far as the universities extend their orbit in response to the demands of the technical branches of industry. (SSEC, 1943, p. 4)

Significantly, the Norwood Report went on to say: 'we have treated secondary education as that phase of education in which differences between pupils receive the consideration due to them' (ibid., p. 4).
   The 1944 Education Act, which played such a major role in determining the principles underpinning the post-war education system, came to be regarded by many commentators as a corner-stone of the Welfare State, though it could be argued that it had a number of weaknesses and shortcomings which undermined its good intentions. It certainly sought to extend educational oppor-tunity by providing free secondary education for all, but it failed to provide a clear definition of the *structure* of secondary education.

The assumptions of the Act, and of the 1943 White Paper *Educational Reconstruction* which preceded it, appeared to favour a tripartite system, though multilateral and comprehensive schools were not officially proscribed. One interpretation of Section 8 of the Act, referring to the provision of opportunities for all pupils 'in view of their different ages, abilities and aptitudes, and of the different periods for which they may be expected to remain at school', ensured that secondary reform of a radical nature was deferred for many years. At the same time, the *ambiguity* in the working of the Act meant that when the pressure for reform became almost irresistible in the 1960s, it could be carried out by *reinterpreting* the Section's formula without the need for further legislation. Attention was, in fact, drawn to this possibility, even while the Bill was under discussion, by an experienced educational administrator, J. Chuter Ede, the Labour Parliamentary Secretary to the Board of Education. 'I do not know where people get the idea about three types of school', he said, in a speech in April 1944, 'because I have gone through the Bill with a small-tooth comb, and I can find only one school for senior pupils, and that is a secondary school. What you like to make of it will depend on the way you serve the precise needs of the individual area in the country' (reported in *The Times*, 14 April 1944).

Yet, despite the advocacy of a tripartite system of secondary schools in official documents, if not in the Act itself, such a structure was never fully realized in practice. In most areas, priority was given to establishing the new system of secondary modern schools, while the majority of local authorities were reluctant to develop secondary technical schools on the scale envisaged in the Norwood Report. This caution may have resulted from a certain amount of confusion as to the exact function of these schools, or it may have been due to the cost of the equipment required. Whatever the reason, as late as 1958, secondary technical schools still accounted for less than four per cent of the secondary age-group. The post-war structure that emerged was, therefore, in reality, a *bi-partite* system comprising grammar schools on the one hand and secondary modern schools on the other – the former taking, in 1950, one in five of all children at the age of eleven.

At the same time, the introduction of new common or comprehensive schools was being actively discouraged. Experimentation was to be restricted to the development of a few multilateral schools where 'grammar' and 'secondary modern' pupils (and sometimes 'technical' as well) would be educated on the same site, while following a curriculum suited to their needs and possibly educated in clearly demarcated buildings. The Ministry further stipulated that multilateral schools must be large establishments of at least 1600 pupils. Circular 144, issued in June 1947, argued that a multi-lateral school must be able to provide effective education of all three types; to do this, it needed as a minimum a ten-form entry of around 300 pupils which could then be divided into two 'grammar' streams, two 'technical' streams and six or seven 'modern' streams. Comprehensive schools, if they were to offer a sufficient variety of courses, must be of a similar size – although the terms 'grammar', 'technical' and 'modern' would not be required (Ministry of Education, 1947, p. 3). When Middlesex proposed a rapid transition to comprehensive education by making use at first of existing buildings, the plan was rejected by the Ministry in 1949 for two main reasons: first, the secondary schools proposed were too small to allow for the creation of a sixth form of adequate size; and, second, the 'logical' way of dealing with different 'types' of children was by providing different 'types' of school. London, on the other hand, was able to press ahead, in 1946/47, with the establishment of five 'interim' comprehensive schools by merging selective central schools with modern schools and making use of existing buildings, each school comprising about 1200 pupils.

It was only in the late 1950s that popular opinion began to move strongly in favour of a new structure of secondary schools, and this was accompanied by profound misgivings about the validity of the eleven-plus selection procedure, a point to which we will now turn in the next chapter.

Chapter 5

Intelligence Testing Challenged

Introduction

In the period immediately following the Second World War, the views of psychometrists and intelligence testers went largely unchallenged. Throughout the country, children at the age of ten or eleven were allocated to one or other of different types of secondary school on the basis of their performance in a selection examination consisting of tests in English, arithmetic and 'intelligence'. Although the precise nature of the selection examination varied from one part of the country to another, according to the predilections of the local education authority concerned, the intelligence test was invariably given double or even treble the weight accorded to any of the other papers. In some areas, the child's primary school record, or the teacher's estimate of his or her 'ability', was taken partially into account. In other parts of the country, some attention was paid to the so-called 'borderline' cases – those who just passed or who just failed – but refinements in selection were rarely concerned with more than just a small minority on the borderline.

When the test papers were marked (usually by teachers at a very low rate of pay), the dividing line between 'pass' and 'fail' was drawn at a certain fixed point, according to the number of grammar school places available in the area concerned. The actual point at which this dividing line was drawn usually varied considerably from area to area – and even sometimes *within* an area. In the West Riding of Yorkshire, for example, the situation in 1952 was such that, in one district, there were grammar school places for 40 per cent of the children; in another, for only 15 per cent. In an article published in 1953, Alec Clegg, Chief Education Officer for the West Riding since 1945, pointed out that:

Under the present system . . . admission may be determined by a fraction of just one per cent. . . . Suppose there are 500 grammar school places to be competed for by 2500 children. The 500th child gets an average mark on all the papers of, say, 60.3 per cent. The 501st gets 60.2 per cent. The cut-off point will then be 60.25 per cent. The former goes to a grammar school; the latter to a modern school. And, of course, just above and just below them will be grouped many other children who share their fate. (Clegg, 1953, p. 9)

Eleven-plus selection not only exerted a decisive influence on the way children were subsequently educated; it also determined the nature of the curriculum and organization of most state junior schools. Not surprisingly, these schools were usually organized, not so much with the aim of providing the best possible education for all the children, as with that of obtaining the greatest number of 'scholarships' or 'passes' in the selection examination at ten or eleven. The tragedy was that many people, including teachers and parents, regarded these two aims as synonymous; whereas they were, of course, mutually exclusive. Speaking in a debate in the House of Commons in February 1953, an MP and former teacher argued that:

Some primary school headmasters [*sic*] have moulded the whole of their curriculum around the grammar school entrance examination. From the time the child comes into the junior school at the age of seven, his attention is directed towards this examination. The whole of the primary school curriculum is distorted and warped . . . and this warping is a very evil thing. (*Hansard*, H of C., Cols. 311–12, 17 February 1953)

With the reputation of primary schools among parents largely dependent on the achievement of a sizeable number of grammar school entrants in each academic year, there was, of course, tremendous pressure on headteachers to make special provision for those considered to be the 'brightest' in their age group. This distortion of the curriculum caused Alex Clegg to note satirically in the article quoted above:

If the Committee for the West Riding were to decide that, henceforth, they would select for grammar schools solely on the children's ability to do long division, this form of calculation would be the main and most serious occupation of certain junior schools for the whole of their four-year course, to the detriment of many other activities which ought to be occupying those years. (ibid., p. 9)

Writing in 1961, educationist and reformer Brian Jackson looked back on his experience of working in a streamed (A, B, C) primary school in the 1950s. Here, *from the outset*, only the 'brightest' children in the 'top' stream had been specially 'groomed' for success in the eleven-plus selection examination. So that selection at *eleven* had become, in effect, selection at *seven*. And such a process was always bound to be arbitrary and unfair. Describing his experience of working with the children in the school, Brian Jackson explained that the more he had got to know and value them all – 'of the grammar school type', 'of the C type', etc. – the more he had become convinced that 'they had not been "given" to us in these "neat" categories: *we had manufactured them*'. In Jackson's view, 'they were the product of the educational society that *we* had established. . . . That society demanded that they be selected or rejected at eleven; therefore we pre-selected at ten, nine, eight, seven, even six' (Jackson, 1961, pp. 6, 8).

Objections to the System

Despite the popular belief in the whole idea of innate intelligence, it was, in fact, in the first half of the 1950s that two books appeared which powerfully attacked the use of intelligence tests as a means of determining a child's future prospects at the age of eleven. Brian Simon's *Intelligence Testing and the Comprehensive School*, published in 1953, argued that intelligence tests not only 'exclude, or attempt to exclude, any emotional response', but also 'isolate the individual from all social relations and any "real life" situation' (Simon, 1953, p. 60). Alice Heim's *The Appraisal of Intelligence*, which appeared the following year, maintained that 'intelligence . . . cannot be separated from other aspects of mental activity', and insisted on the necessity of 'studying intelligence as part of the total personality' (Heim, 1954, p. 1).

Among Brian Simon's many criticisms of intelligence tests, it was argued that 'success' in answering the questions involved a great deal of 'acquired knowledge' and that many of the questions had a built-in social and cultural bias. He used a pre-war test to make his point:

A verbal intelligence test for children of about eleven, chosen at random, shows that in order to have the necessary data to answer some of the questions at all, the testee must know the following things: the meaning of such words as 'spurious', 'antique', 'external', 'irregular', 'inexpensive', 'affectionate', 'moist'; that a sovereign is made of gold, while a florin is made of silver, that pearls, emeralds, sapphires, diamonds and rubies are precious stones, while gold is not; the relative functions of telephone and telegraph; the use of thermometers; the reasons for saving money; the purpose of charitable societies; what a cubic block is; what a code is; what a clerk's job is; that ledger-clerks work in banks; what an individual's 'mechanical bent' is; what a person's 'inclinations' are; that a shorthand-typist is expected to be able to spell well; what 'the adjustment of an individual to his vocation' means; and, finally, that a parlourmaid is not expected to do the sewing in a house! . . . Such knowledge may seem obvious to the adult and even to the 'fortunate' child of eleven, but it is by no means so obvious to the 'average' child brought up in an overcrowded house in the centre of an industrial city. One might say that the information required for success depends directly on *social status*. Many working-class children will never have heard of the subject-matter of some of these questions discussed and yet these questions cannot be answered unless the *meaning* of each of the words is fully grasped. (Simon, 1953, p. 63)[1]

Leslie Hearnshaw has suggested (1979, pp. 59, 227–8) that the books by Brian Simon and Alice Heim, and especially the one by Professor Simon, played a major role in causing Cyril Burt to search for and indeed *fabricate* data in order to substantiate his theories. Thanks largely to the meticulous research carried out by Professor Leon Kamin of Princeton University (see Kamin, 1974), we now have evidence that most of Burt's later work, and particularly his influential papers on identical twins reared apart, had little or no basis in reality; but it is not clear exactly when the psychologist resorted to unorthodox and fraudulent methods to defeat the arguments of his critics. (It is also fair to point out that there are those who argue [see, for example, Wooldridge, 1994] that the attacks against Burt, and particularly the attempts to discredit his theories about innate ability, were motivated by a mixture of professional and ideological antagonism, and that Burt was entirely innocent of the 'malicious charges' levelled against him.)

In the mid-1950s, when Burt's theories about mental inheritance and his fanatical commitment to mass intelligence testing were just beginning to cause disquiet and alarm among sections of the academic and teaching community (and this was 20 years before charges of deliberate deception were made), it was, paradoxically, the development of the divided secondary system itself which played a large role in challenging and undermining the hard-line 'classic' views of the leading psychometrists. In particular, the unexpected passes secured by many secondary modern candidates in the new GCE (General Certificate of Education) Ordinary Level Examination introduced in 1951 had the obvious and immediate effect of exposing the fallibility of the eleven-plus selection procedure. By the end of the 1950s, it had become much more difficult to argue that every child was born with a given quota of 'intelligence' which remained constant throughout his or her life – and that this key quality was a direct product of genetic endowment and not therefore in any way susceptible to the influence of schooling. In other words, it could not be argued that the level of 'intelligence' any child could reach was already determined by biological mechanisms – that a child was born with *all that he or she could become.*[2]

One secondary modern school for girls serving a working-class district in a large industrial city, which took in only those children who had *failed* to gain entrance to either a grammar or a selective central school, entered a number of its sixteen-year-old girls for the GCE Ordinary Level Examination in 1954. Of those who gained five or more passes, one had had an IQ of 97 on entry to the School in 1949; another an IQ of 85. (This was at a time when an IQ of 115 or over was generally considered to be necessary to succeed in examination courses.) And other secondary modern schools were soon in a position to boast of similar achievements, so that there were real problems involved in defending the psychometrists' standpoint (see Simon, 1955, pp. 64–6).

Evidence was also beginning to emerge that the eleven-plus selection process discriminated against girls. In 1954, a front-page story appeared in the *Hunts Post*, the County Paper for Huntingdonshire, under the bold headline: 'Girls Brainier than Boys'. Apparently, too many girls had been 'passing' the eleven-plus examination, and the Education Authority, ignoring the formal protests of teachers, had decided to limit their numbers. 'As a result', the Paper wrote, 'some boys will be admitted to the grammar schools, although their educational performance may well be inferior to that of some of the girls who are excluded' (quoted in Grant, 1994, p. 37). While acknowledging the essential truth of the story, the Scholarship Sub-Committee for the County felt that nothing could be done to make the situation fairer, even though it realized that 'no useful purpose was being served by allowing the admittance of boys who were clearly incapable of taking a grammar-school course' (ibid.).

Other evidence suggests (see, for example, Chitty, 1989, p. 33; Chitty, 2002, pp. 133–4; Plummer, 2000, p. 15) that this was *not* an isolated incident. For many years, most English local education authorities operated a quota system for girls similar to those used by American Ivy League Universities to limit the admission of Jewish and black students to their courses. It seems clear that many 'able' girls who had, in fact, 'passed' the eleven-plus examination were relegated to the local secondary modern school; while boys with lower marks were seen to be marching off to school in the autumn term in their smart grammar-school blazers.

If challenged about this situation, local authorities argued in their defence that if quotas had not been imposed in *mixed* grammar schools, two-thirds of the classrooms would have been occupied by girls. Throughout primary school and in the early years of secondary education, girls performed better on average than did boys in *most*, if not *all*, academic subjects. At that time, the accepted theory held that girls 'matured' earlier than did boys, but that, in the later years of the secondary school, the boys would inevitably catch up. (It is fair to say that this situation no longer seems to apply, so that now we appear to be facing a 'failing boys' phenomenon in many secondary schools.)

It was as a result of all this compelling evidence in the first half of the 1950s that some psychometrists did, in fact, feel obliged to tone down some of their more doctrinaire statements and put forward a modified and more sophisticated view of human intel-lectual capacity. This subtle change of emphasis came in a report of a special working party set up by the British Psychological Society with the intention of responding to some of the well-informed criti-cisms of the practice of universal testing and of the very concept of the IQ examination as an accurate measure of *innate* ability. This Report, published in 1957, conceded that since it was now clear that many pupils could actually *enhance* their IQ scores, it must be true that 'environmental' factors had *some* effect on 'intelligence' – and particularly in the early and teenage years. But although this Report did express reservations about all the claims made for the eleven-plus examination and was also critical of the widespread practice of streaming within the junior school, it had nothing to say about *education* as the key to human development. A refusal to challenge the narrow assumptions of the past meant that only 'heredity' and the vague and generalized category of 'environment' (comprising a wide range of 'active' and 'passive' influences) were recognized as determining factors in a child's intellectual development. As Brian Simon pointed out at the beginning of the 1970s: 'From a theoretical point of view . . . the psychometrists, by abandoning "heredity" for "environment", were merely switching from the roundabout to the swing, without giving any evidence of an intention to leave the fairground' (Simon, 1971, pp. 22–3).

In 1958, a book appeared satirizing the whole idea of using IQ tests to create a new 'meritocracy', a term actually coined by the author of the book and now in common usage. *The Rise of the Meritocracy* by Michael Young set out to show that establishing a meritocracy involved the creation of a new social class whose members believed that their privileges and superior status were thoroughly deserved on account of their undisputed merit, as demonstrated by their above average IQ scores and educational qualifications. While the good intentions of the Government in Lord Young's satire involved separating and distinguishing individual merit from considerations of birth, inherited wealth, nepotism, bribery, patronage or purchase, the rise of the new class of ambitious meritocrats caused all sorts of social problems. The book took the form of a journal written by a hero of the people killed in a violent encounter between the Meritocracy and the Populist Party in 2034 (p. 190); and it described in telling detail how the Government had attempted, by the skilful use of 'scientific testing', to create a radical and progressive meritocracy. The threat from the Left was 'warded off' and the comprehensive school experiment was abandoned (p. 55), as 'able' children were separated from the stupid who went on to become permanent members of the lower classes. The brightest individuals were rewarded for their talent by being able to climb the ladder into the higher class. They acquired new accents and joined BUGSA (the British Union of Grammar School Attenders) (p. 59); while intelligence tests became so refined and sophisticated that all members of the public were required to carry a National Intelligence Card, issued by Eugenics House (p. 89). Unfortunately, the children of Lords were not always happy to find themselves demoted on account of their stupidity, being forced to live in council houses and carry out menial tasks.

Also women were not keen on having to produce their IQ card before marriage. As time went on, a hard core of egalitarians became a danger to the State; while a member of the elite decided to write a pamphlet urging a fair deal for the upper classes called *The Elite's Work is Never Done* (p. 157). Eventually, a populist movement challenged the meritocracy, and the final confrontation took place at Peterloo.[3]

In the 1950s, one of the leading campaigners for the abolition of the eleven-plus examination was Dr Robin Pedley, at that time a colleague of Brian Simon's in the Education Department of the University of Leicester; and in 1963 he produced an influential and widely read Pelican Original, *The Comprehensive School*, which challenged the view that intelligence tests could 'detect and measure inborn ability'. It was Pedley's argument that 'none of the intelligence tests conceived and tried over the course of sixty years' could satisfactorily distinguish 'natural talent' from 'what had been learned'. In Pedley's view, 'heredity and environment were too closely entangled to be clearly identified'. This meant that children from 'literate homes', with 'interested and helpful parents', had an enormous advantage over 'children from culturally poor homes' where books were unknown and conversation was 'either limited or unprintable' (Pedley, 1963, pp. 16–17).

Of even greater significance, the first chapter of the 1963 Newsom Report, *Half Our Future*, a report concerned with the education of 13-to-16-year-old students of 'average or less than average ability', also rejected the idea that it was possible to isolate and measure *innate* ability as something separate from, and ultimately more important than, *acquired* intelligence:

> Intellectual talent is *not* a fixed quantity with which we have to work, but a variable that can be modified by social policy and educational approaches. The crude and simple point was made by Thomas Macaulay in his work *On the Athenian Orators*, published in 1824: 'Genius is subject to the same laws which regulate the production of cotton and molasses. The supply simply adjusts itself to the demand. The quantity may be diminished by restrictions and multiplied by bounties. . . . A more subtle investigation into what constitutes the 'restrictions' and the 'bounties' in our society is of comparatively recent origin. And the results of this investigation increasingly indicate that the kind of intelligence which is measured by the tests so far applied is largely an *acquired* characteristic. This is not to deny the

existence of a basic genetic endowment; but whereas that endowment, so far, has proved impossible to isolate, other factors can be identified. And particularly significant among them are the influences of social and physical environment; and, since these are susceptible to modification, they may well prove educationally more important. (Ministry of Education, 1963, p. 6)

In his Foreword to the Report, Conservative Education Minister Edward Boyle implicitly rejected the standpoint of the psychometrists when he stated that the essential point we have to grasp is that 'all children should have an equal opportunity of acquiring intelligence and of developing their talents and abilities to the full' (ibid., p. iv).

The Plowden Report published in 1967, the Report of a committee chaired by Lady Plowden, which had been set up by Edward Boyle in August 1963 to consider 'the whole subject of primary education and the transition to secondary education', was suffused with a warm humanity, the famous opening sentence of the second chapter of Volume One being 'at the heart of the educational process lies the child' (DES, 1967, p. 7). Human development was described as the result of the complex interaction of a 'heredity tendency' and 'environmental factors' such as the level or degree of 'encouragement or discouragement' children experienced (ibid., p. 18). The adverse effects of eleven-plus selection were highlighted, and, with its emphasis on 'individual learning', the Report came out unequivocally in favour of the abolition of streaming within infant, junior and middle schools (ibid., p. 291). There was nothing to be gained from preparing children from a really early age for a selection process that was itself flawed. And if the child's educational (and other) experiences were to be seen as central to intellectual and indeed to overall development, the 'categorization' or 'streaming' of children according to their *existing* level of development at any point in time simply could not be justified. Instead it was necessary, as far as possible, to provide a rich and stimulating environment for *all* children, giving ample scope for the realization of children's many-sided and exciting potentialities.

By the end of the 1960s, even some of those on the Right of the political spectrum were conceding that the eleven-plus selection test and the divided secondary system which it had underpinned had been deeply flawed. For example: Dr Rhodes Boyson, at that time Headteacher of Highbury Grove Comprehensive School and later a prominent Conservative politician, contributed an article to *Black Paper Two: The Crisis in Education*, published in 1969,[4] articulating some of the reasons why comprehensive reorganization had proved popular in many parts of the country:

> There is no doubt that the eleven-plus tests made considerable mistakes, that very many secondary modern school pupils *can* undertake academic work, and that the arrangements for transfer within the tripartite system were unsatisfactory. My five years as a secondary modern school class teacher and then five as a secondary modern school head convinced me that the view that secondary schools were equal but different was poppy-cock. . . . The only secondary modern schools which approached in status the grammar schools were the ones which copied the grammar school's academic ethic, sat external examinations and, through good discipline, an attractive uniform, some exclusiveness in intake and the creation of tradition, became respected locally. The secondary modern schools with progressive methods, rural science, much art and music and freedom of development endeared themselves to no one other than the vaguely idealistic, unworldly and levitating types so well represented and influential amongst education officials and advisors. (Boyson, 1969, p. 57)

New views about 'intelligence' which gained credibility in the 1950s and 1960s were accompanied by the work of a number of leading sociologists and researchers which found that grammar schools were largely *middle-class* institutions and that streamed primary schools were invariably divided along class lines. These influential sociological studies (notably Glass, 1954; Floud *et al.*, 1956) pointed to a direct relationship between social class and educational opportunities, bringing out clearly the extent to which all aspects of the divided secondary system discriminated against the children of working-class parents and, conversely, favoured the middle-class child. As we saw earlier in the chapter, eleven-plus selection often involved the allocation of children to specific streams or groups as early as the age of seven and this itself had profound *social* implications. The results of a large-scale investigation of children in the primary-school years carried out by the Medical Research Council Unit at the London School of Economics under the leadership of Dr J. W. B. Douglas were reported in *The Home and the School: A Study of Ability and Attainment in the Primary School*, published in 1964, and the researchers concluded that streaming by ability 'reinforced the process of social selection'.

> Children who come from well-kept homes, and who are themselves clean, well-clothed and shod, stand a greater chance of being put in the upper streams than their measured ability would seem to justify. Once there, they are likely to stay and to improve in performance in succeeding years. This is in striking contrast to the deterioration noticed in those children often of similar measured ability who were placed in the lower streams. In this way, the validity of the initial selection appears to be confirmed by the subsequent performance of the children, and an element of rigidity is introduced early in the primary-school system. (Douglas, 1964, p. 150)

The 1967 Plowden Report also concluded that primary-school streaming served as 'a means of social selection', with 'middle-class pupils congregating in the upper streams and the children of semi-skilled and unskilled workers in the lower streams' (DES, 1967, p. 289).

Success in tests in English, arithmetic and 'intelligence' was, of course, possible for a *minority* of working-class pupils; but even here, the outcome was not always satisfactory. The post-war grammar schools were seen by many as the 'custodians' of middle-class values, and in their influential study *Education and the Working Class*, first published in 1962 and based on research undertaken in Huddersfield, Brian Jackson and Dennis Marsden showed that even when children from working-class backgrounds actually gained entry to a local grammar school, they found it an uncomfortable and disorienting experience. In the words of Jackson and Marsden:

> The grammar schools are a glory to the English middle classes, and to the first stages of state education. Their achievement is an honourable one. They are rich in middle-class values. Often good values; and good attitudes; but *not the only ones*, and not in our time always the best. Every custom, every turn of phrase, every movement of judgement, informs the working-class parent and the working-class child that the grammar schools do not 'belong' to them. (Jackson and Marsden, 1962, p. 237)

From so many viewpoints, the post-war divided system, under-pinned by spurious notions of 'intelligence', was seen as having to be drastically modified or perhaps even abandoned altogether. The idea of 'parity of esteem' between grammar and secondary modern schools was, as we have seen, a sham; and 'failure' in the eleven-plus examination was invariably a cause of much distress both for a child and its parents. Writing in 1965, Stewart Mason, the Director of Education for Leicestershire (the county in the Midlands which experimented with a two-tier (11–14, 14–18) comprehensive school scheme as early as 1957) looked back on the previous decade when the life chances of so many young people were destroyed as part of the process of preserving an elite education for the few:

> A sense of success in a few was being paid for by a sense of failure in the many; primary school friendships were severed, brothers and sisters artificially separated. A sense of social injustice was being engendered, while reservoirs of talent were doomed to remain untapped. More and more people were coming to see that the eleven-plus reflected an outmoded 'we/they' society. (Mason, 1965, p. 52)

Historian David Crook has emphasized that 'the drive for comprehensive education in England and Wales as a means of abolishing secondary selection was a "bottom up", rather than a "top down" initiative' (Crook, 2002, p. 257), with the limited local experiments of the 1950s providing the essential background to the remarkable developments of the following decade. The local elections of May 1963, held at a time when the Conservative Party had been in power for almost twelve years, resulted in sweeping victories for the Labour Party and provided a vital catalyst for the growing comprehensive movement. Bristol, Liverpool and Manchester LEAs swiftly produced city-wide schemes for comprehensive reorganization; while the London County Council finally felt able to abandon the eleven-plus examination, replacing it in those areas where grammar schools continued to exist by a combination of teacher assessment and parental choice. A number of rural counties, including Devon, Dorset and Shropshire, none of them Labour controlled, also declared themselves in favour of the introduction of comprehensive education.

The grass-roots movement that was in progress in the early 1960s demanded a new approach to education from a Conservative government that seemed to be losing popular support where the issue of secondary selection was concerned. The Minister of Education Edward Boyle (1962-4) did not share the hostility of the majority of his parliamentary colleagues towards comprehensive schooling and began encouraging local education authorities to look at viable strategies for softening their selection procedures – in a vain attempt to forestall more drastic solutions. In a private briefing paper to Prime Minister Harold Macmillan, dated 3 July 1963, he recommended that the Conservative Government should 'make an end of the strict neutrality which my Department has maintained in public towards local selection methods' (quoted in Crook, 2002, p. 251).

In the event, 13 years of unbroken Conservative rule came to an end when Harold Wilson's Labour Party was returned to power in the October 1964 General Election with a meagre majority of just *four* over the other political parties. In the early months of this new Government, it was decided that implementation of the policy of secondary reorganization in England and Wales should take the form of a Circular to be issued to all 163 local education authorities. This was still the period when the education system could be fairly described as 'a central service, locally administered'. We know that after Anthony Crosland became Education Secretary in January 1965, there was a fierce debate within the Department of Education and Science as to whether the new Circular should *require* or *request* the local authorities to prepare plans for reorganization, but there was general agreement that the dismantling of local autonomy was certainly not a process to be undertaken lightly. Interviewed by Professor Maurice Kogan at the end of 1970, Crosland claimed that, in deciding to back those of his officials opting for 'request', he had been strongly influenced both by his meetings with the Association of Education Committees and by his judgement of 'the general mood of the local authority world' (see Kogan, 1971, p. 189). Large numbers of Labour and Conservative authorities seemed to be broadly sympathetic to what the Government was proposing, and there seemed little point in risking widespread alienation by adopting a policy of compulsion.

In a speech delivered at the end of May 1965, Crosland defended his conciliatory policy by reminding his audience that almost two-thirds of the secondary school population already lived in areas where the local authority was implementing or planning a comprehensive schools policy:

> The fact is that there has been a growing movement against the eleven-plus examination – and all that it implies. This movement has not been politically inspired or imposed from the Centre. It

has been a spontaneous growth at the grass roots of education, leading to the widespread conviction that separation is an offence against the child as well as a brake on social and economic progress. . . . The whole notion of a selection test at the age of eleven belongs to the era when secondary education was a privilege of the few, and this is now generally understood. (quoted in Kerckhoff *et al.*, 1996, p. 28)

The Psychometrists Fight Back

Despite growing popular opposition to the eleven-plus selection examination and mounting grass-roots support for comprehensive reorganization, there were still a number of diehard eugenicists and psychometrists in the 1950s and 1960s who remained committed to the idea of innate, mental ability and to the desirability of using intelligence tests for the purpose of allocating children to various types of secondary school at the age of ten or eleven. Cyril Burt, Hans Eysenck and Richard Lynn were prominent among those who were determined to mount a counter-offensive against current 'progressive' trends in educational and social thinking.

In an article published in 1959, Cyril Burt reiterated his view of the essential rationale for the eleven-plus examination:

It is essential, in the interests alike of the children themselves and of the nation as a whole, that those who possess the highest ability – the cleverest of the clever – should be identified as accurately as possible. Of the methods hitherto tried out, the so-called eleven-plus exam has proved to be by far the most trust-worthy. (Burt, 1959, p. 117, quoted in Gould, 1981, p. 293)

Cyril Burt, Hans Eysenck and Richard Lynn all contributed articles to *Black Paper Two: The Crisis in Education*, published in 1969. Burt's piece entitled 'The mental differences between children' not only reiterated Francis Galton's view that mental differences were wholly or largely inherited, but also argued that, owing to recent 'progressive' education reforms carried out by the Wilson Government, standards in basic education were lower than they had been 55 years earlier, in the period just before the outbreak of the First World War (Burt, 1969, p. 23). The article by Hans Eysenck, Professor of Psychology at London University, with the title 'The rise of the mediocracy', argued that the abolition of eleven-plus selection would deny to large numbers of working-class children the possibility of social advancement and would bring to the top of society 'a large number of people of *mediocre* ability, while keeping submerged many people of *superior* ability'. This rise of a new mediocracy would be 'socially unjust, nationally disastrous and ethically unacceptable' (Eysenck, 1969, p. 40). The third article, by Richard Lynn, Research Professor of Psychology at Dublin University, was perhaps the most provocative of the three. In this contribution, entitled 'Comprehensives and equality', Professor Lynn highlighted some of the 'lies' perpetrated by 'radical progressives' (referred to in the article as 'young red guards'):

> One of the most serious of these lies is that it is somehow the fault of society that our slum dwellers are impoverished and their children do badly in school. To the young red guards, it follows that society is unjust and must be overthrown. They do not realize that slum dwellers are caused principally by low innate intelligence and poor family upbringing, and that the real social challenge is posed by this. (Lynn, 1969, p. 30)

It was also in 1969 that Professor Arthur Jensen (a pupil of Hans Eysenck, who had himself been one of Cyril Burt's postgraduate students) published a famous (or rather notorious) article in America widening the debate about 'intelligence' to embrace issues of 'race'; and it is with this publication in the *Harvard Educational Review*, that we begin the next chapter.

Chapter 6

The New Preoccupation with Intelligence and 'Race'[1]

The Persistent Popularity of Eugenic theories

As we have seen in previous chapters, the popularity and status of eugenic theories came to be seriously undermined by revelations after 1945 of atrocities committed in the name of 'science' by Adolf Hitler and his followers during the period of Nazi government in Germany beginning in 1933. Yet several decades after the end of the Second World War, it was still possible to find a minority of educationists and politicians putting forward ideas about education and society which had profound eugenic and racist implications. These ideas, though often based on flawed data and a set of equally dubious assumptions, soon exerted a powerful influence on policy-makers on both sides of the Atlantic.

It was in 1969, the year that saw the launch of the first two Black Papers in Britain, that Arthur Jensen, Professor of Psychology at the University of California, published his controversial article in America in the *Harvard Educational Review* entitled 'How much can we boost IQ and scholastic achievement?' (Jensen, 1969). This very long paper, running to over 120 pages, soon acquired considerable notoriety because it set out to reiterate Cyril Burt's theory of fixed innate intelligence in terms not only of 'class' but also of 'race'. It began with the bold assertion that compensatory education had been tried and had failed. In particular, it had failed to improve the scores on IQ tests of 'underprivileged children' – and especially of black children. As measured by standard IQ tests, the scores of black children were apparently an average of 15 points below those of white children. According to Jensen, 'environmentalists' who had argued in favour of massive compensatory education programmes designed to equalize opportunities had been guilty of seriously misleading the American Government. As a consequence, resources had been wasted and a great deal of effort expended on a pointless exercise. In Jensen's view, just as working-class white children were inferior (in terms of measured intelligence) to middle- and upper-class white children, so black children were innately inferior to white children. Any attempt, however well-intentioned, to compensate for this 'natural' state of affairs was obviously a waste of time and money.

Somewhat inevitably, Jensen's main conclusions received wide publicity in America; and they were treated as if they were *scientific* findings, rather than hypotheses which he was advancing for examination and discussion, as, to be fair, he himself insisted. Their practical and political significance immediately became apparent when his views were quoted by lawyers in the Deep South of the United States in the campaign against integration in the schools. It was now argued that there should be all-black 'remedial' schools for 'backward' black pupils, with black children admitted to white schools only if they passed a number of demanding standardized intelligence tests. In other words, segregation, far from being seen as something to be abolished, was now to be 'streamlined' on 'scientific' grounds. In the words of Professor Lawler, Professor of Philosophy at the State University of New York, it was obvious to many people that 'segregated schools were inherently unequal', and, in addition, they had detrimental consequences for the wellbeing of *both* black *and* white children: 'while perpetuating inferior education for black children, they also condemned white children to the backward cultural isolation in which poisonous racist ideas could easily breed'. As Lawler puts it, 'the theory perpetuated by Jensen . . . located inequality and educational inferiority in the genes of the victims of racism themselves, and declared nature itself to be the first cause and champion of segregation' (Lawler, 1978, p. 4).

Throughout the United States, Jensen's article gave rise to heated debates among politicians, scientists and those professionally engaged in education. The two subsequent numbers of the *Harvard Educational Review* were filled with articles and correspondence, primarily in protest, but also occasionally in support; and Jensen later replied in detail to some of the criticisms raised.

The Jensen thesis also made the front pages of newspapers in Britain, but the articles were not always well-informed; and it was not until the publication of the May 1969 number of the *New Scientist*, a popular but serious weekly journal, that there occurred the first balanced evaluation of Jensen's ideas. Introducing the discussion, the Editorial referred to 'the storm of protests and invective' which had greeted Jensen's thesis in the States, pointing out that his controversial views had 'struck political dynamite'. It went on to link the matter with current social and educational issues in Britain:

> Professor Arthur Jensen makes the claim that US Negroes are less intelligent than their white countrymen. Haringey Education Committee's decision to distribute immigrant children on the supposition that they are less intelligent than British pupils, and recent pronouncements by Lord Snow and others,[2] have all focused attention on the emotive subject of intelligence and 'race'.

To the Editor of the *New Scientist*, it was clear that, in the resultant controversy, 'science, politics and prejudice have become inextricably mixed' (*New Scientist*, 1 May 1969, p. 1).

A major development in the debate came in July 1970 when Arthur Jensen visited England to address two large meetings in Cambridge, one organized by the Brain Research Association, the other by the Cambridge Society for Social Responsibility in Science (CSSRS). This CSSRS open meeting was specifically arranged because of the social and political implications of Jensen's thesis and because of the failure to report the scientific objections to his arguments. It was, in fact, widely reported, and the Society later published the proceedings in full. The Editorial in the CSSRS Bulletin explained the reasons for holding the meeting:

> The segregationalists of the southern United States, the Powellite element of the Tory Party,[3] and the 'more-means-worse' authors of the recent Black Papers on Education have all used the 'scientific' evidence of Professor Jensen's article to bolster their political aims. In contrast to their uncritical acceptance and that of the popular press, Professor Jensen's views have not received much support among his fellow scientists. Many eminent psychologists, geneticists and educationalists have been provoked to produce rebuttals and protests, but, as is usual, these have been accorded far less publicity than the original article. . . . All this explains the need for this important meeting. (quoted in Simon, 1971, p. 247)

In the event, all the contributors to the discussion at the CSSRS meeting – from essentially allied disciplines – were highly critical, many referring to the extraordinary complexity of genetical differences and their assessment, since each individual was now estimated to possess thousands of genes, and pointing out that no general statement could be made about the assignment of fixed proportions to the contributions of heredity and environment *either* to the development of a single individual *or* to the differences among members of a population.

In October 1974, Sir Keith Joseph – from 1981 to 1986 Secretary of State for Education under Margaret Thatcher – included the distinctly 'eugenic' sentence 'the balance of our population, of our human stock, is being threatened' in a now notorious speech on class and intelligence delivered to the Edgbaston Conservative Association in Birmingham's Grand Hotel. The Speech had, in fact, been advertised in the local press as 'offering a night out which will linger in your memory for ever'; though it is likely that its long-term effects were far greater than Sir Keith himself intended, and it certainly ended his chance of standing for the Leadership of the Conservative Party in 1975. The Speech achieved its notoriety because it appeared to be arguing that the nation was moving towards degeneration on account of the high and rising proportion of children being born to mothers, both white and black, 'least fitted to bring children into the world'. In the words of the Speech:

> These are the mothers who were first pregnant in adolescence in social classes four and five (the unskilled and lower skilled). Many of these girls are unmarried; many are deserted or divorced, or soon will be. . . . Some are of low intelligence; most of low educational attainment. They are unlikely to be able to give their children the stable emotional background, the consistent combination of love and firmness which is more important than riches. They are producing problem children, the future unmarried mothers, delinquents, denizens of our borstals, subnormal educational establishments, prisons, hostels for drifters. Yet these mothers, the under-twenties in many cases, single parents from classes four and five, are now producing a third of all births. A high proportion of these births are a tragedy for the mother, the child and for us. . . . If we do nothing, the nation moves towards degeneration, however many resources we pour into preventive work and into the over-burdened educational system. (reported in *The Sunday Times*, 20 October 1974; see also Denham and Garnett, 2001, pp. 265–76)

Sir Keith went on to propose that birth control facilities should be extended to the destitute, poor and inadequate, though some of his right-wing supporters argued that forcible sterilization was the only logical solution to the problems he was highlighting. One Labour MP summarized the message of the Speech as 'castrate or conform'.

Black immigrants and the 'mentally retarded' were clearly the two principal targets of eugenicists and their followers in Britain in the 1960s and 1970s. Professor Roy Lowe has argued that 'eugenic ideas were, in fact, used throughout the twentieth century to legit-imate social class distinctions and, in their extreme form, to support suggestions that sterilization policies might be used to deal with the problem of what was then called "degeneracy"'. In Professor Lowe's view, 'it was the reapplication of these essentially eugenic ideas to "race", and their survival after the Second World War and the Holocaust, which went a long way to explain the ways in which the education system came, in practice, to bolster the position of so-called "indigenous" white citizens'. Education, then, was one of the agencies through which ethnicity came to be seen as one of the tokens of social class. It seems clear to Professor Lowe that 'the racialization of education in the 1960s and 1970s, and, with it, the marginalization of ethnic minorities, reflected – despite many claims to the contrary – the new eugenics which had come to underpin many aspects of social policy' (Lowe, 1997, pp. 4, 110).

In the 1960s, a number of local authorities, notably Bradford, West Bromwich and Southall, adopted the policy of 'bussing', whereby a minority of black and minority ethnic pupils were 'bussed' into predominantly 'white' areas to prevent the emergence of all-black, inner-city schools. The obvious difficulties involved in implementing such a policy meant that it was never adopted on a widespread basis, although the Department for Education and Science was still defending it as a viable way forward as late as 1971. Its total abandonment in the mid-1970s was widely welcomed by immigrant community leaders, although it meant that the trend towards all-black inner-city primary and secondary schools now continued unabated.[4]

The prevalence of an essentially 'eugenic' view of human society and of intellectual development had a marked effect on the British education system which obviously tended to reflect the deepening divisions in Britain from the 1950s onwards. The majority of teachers saw it as their responsibility to bring about the *assimilation* of newly arrived immigrant pupils into a way of life which, it went without saying, was thought to be in so many ways superior to that which these children had left behind. And a policy of assimilation was the one endorsed by all government ministers, both Conservative and Labour, in the post-war period.

As the 1960s progressed, it was clear that not *all* politicians wanted to see all black immigrants initiated into a common British culture. In a widely reported address to members of the National Committee for Commonwealth Immigrants, delivered on 23 May 1966, Labour Home Secretary and Birmingham MP Roy Jenkins appeared to presage a move away from a crude policy of assimilation when he observed that Britain was entering a new era, 'a move away from the era of the first generation immigrant to that of the second generation immigrant'. In this changing society, he argued, the national aim with regard to Britain's black population should be integration. He went on:

> Integration is perhaps a rather loose word. I do not regard it as meaning the loss, by immigrants, of their own national charac-teristics and culture. I do not think that we need in this country a 'melting pot', which will turn everybody out in a common mould, as one of a series of carbon copies of someone's misplaced vision of the stereotyped Englishman. . . . I define integration . . . not as a flattening process of assimilation, but as equal opportunity, accompanied by cultural diversity, in an atmosphere of mutual tolerance. This is the goal. (quoted in Grosvenor, 1997, pp. 55–6)

It was in this spirit that the Local Government Act of 1966 provided local authorities with supplementary funding to cope with 'the presence within their areas of substantial numbers of immigrants whose language and customs are different from the rest of the community'. This 'Section 11 money', as it came to be known, enabled local authorities and schools to launch a variety of initia-tives designed to deal with the 'problems' posed by minority ethnic pupils. And in the following year (1967) a number of Educational Priority Areas were designated to 'interrupt the cycle of depri-vation' and as part of a policy of 'positive discrimination' for those living in the more deprived areas of the country's large cities.

If assimilation was the guiding policy of the 1950s and 1960s, multiculturalism was to be the rallying cry of the 1970s and 1980s. The 1975 Bullock Report, *A Language for Life*, was strongly multi-culturalist in tone, arguing that 'no child should be expected to cast off the language and culture of the home as he [*sic*] crosses the school threshold' (DES, 1975, p. 453). Then the DES Green Paper *Education in Schools: A Consultative Document*, published in July 1977, argued that, in the previous 20 years, education in Britain had had to adapt to 'sweeping social changes'. Britain had ceased to be 'the centre of an Empire', and had become instead 'a medium-sized European power, albeit one with wide international connections and responsibilities'. It was clear that 'the education appropriate to our Imperial past' could no longer meet 'the requirements of modern Britain' (DES, 1977, p. 4). And it also followed that the curriculum in schools had to reflect 'the needs of the new Britain':

> Our society is now a multicultural, multiracial one, and the curriculum should reflect a sympathetic understanding of the different cultures and races that now make up our society. We live in a complex, interdependent world, and many of our problems in Britain require international solutions. The curriculum should . . . reflect our need to know about and understand other countries. (ibid., p. 41)

If the multicultural movement had a 'bible' or 'manifesto', this was the Swann Report, *Education for All*, published in March 1985. This was the Final Report of the Committee set up in March 1979 by Labour Secretary of State for Education Shirley Williams to inquire into the education of children from ethnic minority groups. Although it made a number of references to the need for anti-racist policies, it was concerned chiefly to endorse the primacy of culture as a key exploration of social/racial relations.

The Report argued strongly that 'a broadly-based "multicultural" approach to the Curriculum' should be adopted by *all* schools, both 'those with ethnic minority pupils' and 'all-white schools'. It did not believe that schooling should seek to 'iron out the differences between cultures', or attempt to 'draw everyone into the dominant culture', but, rather, should 'draw upon the experiences of the many cultures that make up our society and thus broaden the cultural horizons of every child'. In both primary and secondary schools, headteachers and teachers, and 'especially those from ethnic minority groups', were seen as having a vital role to play in encouraging 'a multicultural approach throughout compulsory education' (DES, 1985, p. xx).

In the first chapter, on 'The Nature of Society', the Report contained a powerful affirmation of 'cultural pluralism' as the desired goal for society in Britain:

We consider that a multi-racial society such as ours would, in fact, function most effectively and harmoniously on the basis of pluralism, which enables, expects and encourages members of all ethnic groups, both minority and majority, to participate fully in shaping the society as a whole within a framework of commonly accepted values, practices and procedures, whilst also allowing and, where necessary, helping the various ethnic minority communities to maintain their distinct ethnic identities within this common framework. (ibid., p. 5)

It then went on to conclude this section in the chapter devoted to 'The Concept of Pluralism' with a variation of the above sentiments in the form of a definition of 'a genuinely pluralist society':

We would . . . regard a democratic pluralist society as one seeking to achieve a balance between, on the one hand, the maintenance and active support of the essential elements of the cultures and lifestyles of all the ethnic groups within it, and, on the other, the acceptance by all groups of a set of shared values distinctive of the society as a whole. This, then, is our view of a genuinely pluralist society, as both socially cohesive and culturally diverse. (ibid., p. 6)

The policy of multiculturalism advocated by the 1985 Swann Report was seen by many commentators as having a large number of positive and progressive features, but its implementation in many pioneering primary and secondary schools was also criticized by some for being essentially 'tokenistic'. And it was precisely this dissatisfaction with the basic limitations of the multicultural approach that led a number of schools to embrace the more powerful and proactive focus known as 'anti-racism' – a set of agreed strategies designed to combat racism both in the curriculum and in all the broader aspects of school life. In a wider context, this new approach was characterized by a refusal to accept the existing power relations between black and white people in Britain and was determined to challenge oppression in all its forms.

Leading members of the Thatcher Governments in the 1980s – including the Prime Minister herself – and their Far Right supporters detested *both* multicultural policies *and* anti-racist initiatives in education. As Ian Grosvenor has pointed out: 'the development of local policies to address "race equality" issues in education and other areas of social life was not matched at the national level by any shift away from policies of assimilation. Indeed, the early 1980s were a time *both* of interesting initiatives at the local level *and* of the return of a much more virulent assertion of assimilationist principles by Tory education ministers' (Grosvenor, 1997, p. 70). These principles were invariably articulated around the need to celebrate and promote 'national' values and beliefs. The fundamental values of 'mainstream' white British society were held by the Far Right to be impervious to change or improvement. Commenting in 1983 on the proposed criteria for the new GCSE examinations in history, Secretary of State for Education Keith Joseph asserted: 'one of the aims of studying history is to understand the development of the shared values which are a distinctive feature of British society and culture and which continue to shape both private attitudes and public policy' (reported in *The Times Educational Supplement*, 15 April 1983). And similar sentiments were expressed in 1984 by Junior Education Minister Robert Dunn in a speech to local Conservatives in Ruislip:

> By all means let families foster and teach the language, customs and religion of their former homeland. But it is essential that our schools should foster and teach the language of this, their adopted homeland. Our duty is clear. Whatever else we may also do in our schools, we must teach English and using English, we must teach British history, customs and Christianity. Thus, we will avoid the perpetuation of two classes of citizen. (reported in *The Times Educational Supplement*, 23 November 1984)

Keith Joseph rejected most of the key recommendations of the Swann Report; and, in his valedictory speech as Secretary of State for Education, he condemned the values underpinning both multicultural and anti-racist education. In a long and wide-ranging critique of current thinking, he attacked 'the self-appointed apostles of anti-racism', who 'sought to subvert our fundamental values and institutions' and were 'more anxious to pursue their own political advantage than to create harmony between the various ethnic groups'. There might, he conceded, be a limited place in schools for acknowledging 'the culture and backgrounds of ethnic minority children' – it could possibly promote 'self-confidence' and 'self-esteem' – but it was 'quite unnecessary to turn our education system upside down to accommodate ethnic variety'. He went on:

these ethnic minority children will be for most of their lives in this country. They are British Citizens: this is their home. British history and cultural traditions are . . . part of the common heritage of all who live in this country. . . . Education must ensure that all children have full and equal access to that heritage, so that they can understand the society in which we all live. . . . Schools should obviously be responsible for trying to transmit British culture; while the main responsibility for trans-mitting the minority cultures lies with the homes of the minority communities themselves. (Joseph, 1986, quoted in Grosvenor, 1997, p. 75)

The Swann Report also came under heavy criticism from the New Right pressure group the Hillgate Group,[5] whose second influential pamphlet *The Reform of British Education: From Principles to Practice* was published in September 1987 (Hillgate Group, 1987). In this publication, the Group condemned the Report for condoning 'the desire to lock ethnic minorities within their own languages and customs and to isolate them from the greater society of which they form a part'. According to the Group, acceptance by those on the Left of the Report's principal recommendations went 'hand-in-hand' with a tendency to denounce as 'racists' all those teachers who counted the English language, British history and our national culture as things which it was 'their first duty to impart'. The Report was characterized as representing 'a powerful current of opinion within the educa-tional establishment, a current which, because it engages our post-colonial guilt-feelings, threatens to destroy altogether the basis of our national race and culture'. In its final words on the subject, the pamphlet argued that:

Nothing is more important, in the present period of our history, than to reconcile our minorities, to integrate them into the national culture, and to ensure a common political loyalty, independent of race, creed or colour. Not every national culture can breed such a loyalty; but ours, being part of the universalist culture of Europe, is equal to the task, and must not be sacri-ficed for the sake of a misguided relativism, or out of a misplaced concern for those who might not yet be aware of our culture's strengths and advantages. (ibid., p. 4)

The 'Exposure' of Cyril Burt

Continued interest in eugenic theories relating to 'race' and class coincided with a period when Cyril Burt's competence and integrity underwent a marked reappraisal. It was, in fact, very soon after his death in October 1971 that Burt's work was subjected to detailed criticism by a number of eminent psychologists and educationists; and it was his studies of identical and non-identical twins supposedly separated at birth and then reared apart that caused the most concern. The validity of these influential twin studies was first questioned by Dr Leon Kamin of Princeton University in a colloquium held in the Psychology Department at the University in April 1972. And Kamin's damaging attack then reached a wider audience with the publication in October 1974 of his book *The Science and Politics of IQ* (Kamin, 1974). In this book, Dr Kamin minutely dissected the major studies carried out by Burt and others purporting to demonstrate the heritability of the IQ and found inadequacies and shortcomings in all of them. He argued that the assumption of genetic determination of IQ variation was quite unwarranted, and that there were no justifiable grounds for rejecting the environmentalist hypothesis. Turning to Burt's twin studies, his criticisms fell under four main headings: firstly, there was a lack of precise details as to the methods used to collect the data and as to the populations tested; secondly, there were conflicting and mutually contradictory statements in the various reports and articles; thirdly, there were careless errors in Burt's tables; and finally, and perhaps most damaging of all, there were remarkable, and indeed wholly incredible, consistencies in the correlation coefficients derived from changing sample sizes.

Then a curious advertisement appeared in the Personal Columns of *The Times* of 16 October 1976 which read: '*Sir Cyril Burt.* Could Margaret Howard or J. Conway who helped Sir Cyril Burt in studies of the intelligence of twins, or anyone else who knows them, telephone (reverse charges) Oliver Gillie, 01-485 8953.' It transpired that Oliver Gillie was, in fact, the Medical Correspondent of *The Sunday Times*, and on the front page of that paper eight days later (24 October 1996) appeared an article with the sensational headline: 'Crucial data was faked by eminent psychologist', with, alongside the article, a photograph of Cyril Burt himself. The opening sentence of Gillie's piece set the tone of the whole article:

The most sensational charge of scientific fraud this century is being levelled against the late Sir Cyril Burt, father of British educational psychology. Leading scientists are convinced that Burt published false data and invented crucial facts to support his controversial theory that intelligence is largely inherited.

Gillie's article went on to level four main charges against Burt: firstly, that he often guessed parental IQs and then treated his 'guesses' as hard scientific data; secondly, there was no evidence that the two women, Margaret Howard and J. Conway, who were supposed to have collaborated with Burt on the research for his twin studies, ever actually existed; thirdly, that the concordant correlations identified by Dr Kamin could have been arrived at only by working backwards to make the observations fit the answers; and finally, that Burt clearly fabricated his data to fit the predictions of his favoured genetic theories. Moreover, the gravity of these charges was magnified, in Gillie's view, by reason of the profound influence which Burt's work had exercised on the establishment of selective secondary education in Britain and on pronouncements about racial differences in intelligence by Hans Eysenck and Arthur Jensen. If Burt's statistics were indeed faked, it was a matter not only of *scientific* but also of *political* and *public* concern. The story was taken up by *The Times* on the following day (25 October 1976), with the headline: 'Theories of IQ pioneer completely discredited', and this piece went much further than Gillie's article in claiming not only that the whole idea that intelligence was largely determined by heredity had now been undermined, but also that most of Burt's earlier work dating back to 1909 was equally suspect.[6]

It is not easy to know exactly *when* Burt began to fabricate his data; and it is important to reiterate that there are those who argue (see, for example, Wooldridge, 1994) that the attacks against him have been motivated by a mixture of professional and ideological antagonism and that he was entirely innocent of the charges of fictitious research and data falsification. Burt's official biographer, Professor L. S. Hearnshaw (and he was asked to carry out the work by Burt's own sister) came to the reluctant conclusion that many of the charges levelled against Burt's later work were valid, and that the psychologist was certainly guilty of deception in the matter of the spurious data on separated identical ('monozygotic') twins. Hearnshaw also argues that Burt fabricated the figures on declining levels of scholastic achievement which appeared in his article in the second Black Paper, *The Crisis in Education*, published in 1969 (Burt, 1969) (see Chapter 5). In the circumstances, one might be forgiven for thinking that Hearnshaw's overall judgement on Burt's work and career, which is reproduced below, is somewhat over-generous:

> It would be tempting to . . . maintain with Dr Kamin that all Burt's work from the beginning was scientifically worthless, and then to dismiss him . . . simply as 'a fraudulent scientist', particularly as examples of Burt's devious behaviour in personal and professional relationships would appear to support an all-inclusive condemnation. Nevertheless, such a judgment would be one-sided, and less than just. It would fail to account for the esteem in which Burt was held, almost, if not quite, universally in the early stages of his career, and by many up to the time of his death. It would elevate the judgement of persons who knew him slightly, or not at all, over that of those who were intimately associated with him the days of his prime. It would disregard the assessments of contemporary experts in their appraisal of his work, and it would give insufficient weight to his many scholarly and practical achievements. (Hearnshaw, 1979, p. 259)

The Introduction of New Forms of Selection

In the early 1980s, the Thatcher Government (1979–90) was surprised and dismayed by the opposition it faced to its plans to reintroduce eleven-plus selection in key areas of the country – particularly from those middle-class parents who lived in residential areas served by popular, oversubscribed comprehensive schools. Frustrated by the failure to bring back grammar schools in Solihull and elsewhere, Education Secretary Keith Joseph (in office from 1981 to 1986) emphasized that he was determined to find ways of introducing differentiation into the education system. Interviewed by Brian Walden on ITV's *Weekend World* programme in February 1984, he stressed the need for the provision of separate educational routes and destinations *within* the comprehensive school. 'If it be so, as it is, that selection *between* schools is largely out', he said, apparently conceding defeat on this issue, 'then I emphasize that there *must* be differentiation *within* schools' (reported in *The Times Educational Supplement*, 17 February 1984). All this appeared to reflect the Conservative Government's ready acceptance of the eugenic philosophy enshrined in the 1943 Norwood Report that all children could indeed be divided into specific and easily delineated ability groups (see Chitty, 1987, p. 14).

In fact, of course, even though Brian Walden made no attempt to contradict him, Keith Joseph was quite wrong to suggest in his *Weekend World* interview that selection *between* schools was largely a thing of the past. He was ignoring the existence of the independent sector which catered for around seven per cent of the secondary-school population and the fact that, even after several decades of comprehensive reorganization, there were still around 160 grammar schools in England and Wales, concentrated in English counties such as Buckinghamshire, Kent and Lincolnshire and in many of the larger conurbations. Even in Solihull itself, where the Government hoped to reintroduce eleven-plus selection, there was already a considerable degree of differentiation *between* schools, since the comprehensive system was based on clearly defined catchment areas which served to ensure that the idea of local or 'community' schools meant each school serving a relatively homogeneous social class intake. As Walford and Jones pointed out in an article published in 1986 (Walford and Jones, 1986), children from the affluent middle-class areas in the south of the borough were well catered for, attending prestigious secondary schools well supported by active parent-teacher associations. There was certainly no social mixing with the Birmingham overspill children living in the north of the borough who had a choice of schools that did not enjoy a particularly high reputation. In fact, a number of the working-class families living in the north of the borough actually endorsed the idea of the return of eleven-plus selection in that it might enable albeit a small proportion of their children to attend one or other of the popular schools in the south of the borough – which would obviously become grammar schools under any plans for secondary reorganization.

In the 1980s, a number of radio and television programmes also explored the tendency for secondary schools, particularly in the large cities, to be categorized according to the class of children they served, with marked implications for the perpetuation of selection and differentiation. For example, in a BBC TV *Panorama* programme, 'Schools: selling the children short', shown in March 1986, Margaret Jay revealed the three-tier structure of secondary schools that had developed in many areas of Britain: a top tier consisting of well-endowed, well-resourced private schools; a middle tier embracing comprehensive schools with prosperous middle-class catchment areas and parents able to find the money for expensive books and equipment; and a bottom tier invariably serving large working-class estates where school buildings were often crumbling and books were scarce.[7]

As far as the creation of differentiation *within* the curriculum and structure of comprehensive schools was concerned, the Government's main innovation in the 1980s was the introduction of the TVEI (Technical and Vocational Education Initiative), funded from *outside* education by the Manpower Services Commission.

The TVEI Programme was actually launched by the Prime Minister herself in a House of Commons written statement in November 1982, and was designed, in the words of the accompanying Department of Employment Press Release, 'to stimulate technical and vocational education for 14-to-18 year-olds as part of a drive to improve our performance in the development of new skills and technology' (DoE, 1982, p. 1). After months of detailed preparation and prolonged discussion with a number of sympathetic local education authorities, the Initiative was finally introduced in the form of fourteen local authority pilot projects using a number of carefully selected schools in the Autumn of 1983. The additional financial resources that accompanied adoption of the Scheme proved very attractive to schools and colleges; and by the time Keith Joseph left office in May 1986, the TVEI Project involved 65,000 students in as many as 600 institutions, all working on two- or four-year programmes designed to stimulate work-related education, make the curriculum for some students more 'relevant' to post-school life and enable these students to aim for nationally recognized qualifications in a wide range of technical and vocational subject areas.

Although the TVEI Programme was clearly seen by Conservative education and employment ministers as a useful *differentiating* strategy for secondary schools, there was, in fact, considerable confusion as to the exact *nature* of the intended target-group. Education Secretary Keith Joseph saw the Initiative as having special significance and relevance for the 'lower half' of the 'ability range'. And in discussing the ideal target-group for the Scheme in a BBC TV *Panorama* programme 'Good enough for your child?', broadcast in February 1983, he made specific reference to:

the very large proportion of our children who are not getting a benefit from secondary school. They're certainly not getting a parity of esteem. They're either dropping out, or they're emerging from school without what they themselves, their parents or their future potential employers would expect them to have got at school. . . . These are the children who will benefit from the Government's new vocational plans.[8]

David Young, on the other hand, who, as Chairperson of the Manpower Services Commission played a leading role in devising the Initiative, clearly did not see it as being intended for either the *most* or the *least* able students. Shortly after the Prime Minister's initial announcement, he said that TVEI courses would be aimed at 'the 15 to 85 percentiles of the ability range in schools' (quoted in *Education*, 19 November 1982, p. 386). Later he again argued that the TVEI Scheme was *not* designed for students who were expected to gain 'good' O- and A-levels: 'They are not going to join the Scheme. My main concern is for those who are bright and able but haven't been attracted by academic subjects' (reported in *Education*, 24 December 1982, p. 490). Upon his appointment as Secretary of State for Employment in a Cabinet reshuffle in September 1985, David Young outlined his vision of the future:

> My idea is that, at the end of the decade, there is a world in which 15 per cent of our young go into higher education . . . roughly the same proportion as now. Another 30 to 35 per cent will stay on doing the TVEI, along with other courses, ending up with a mixture of vocational and academic qualifications and skills. The remainder, about half, will simply go on to a two-year YTS (Youth Training Scheme). (reported in *The Times*, 4 September 1985)

This would seem to be a clear statement of the role of the TVEI in David Young's concept of secondary and tertiary tripartism. It also shows us, yet again, how the wartime vision of 'three types of mind' survived virtually intact into the closing decades of the century.

Chapter 7

The Durability of Eugenic Theories

The Situation in America since 1990

Eugenic ideas about human ability and intelligence continued to be popular and influential in America until the very end of the twentieth century, and 1994 saw the publication of *The Bell Curve: Intelligence and Class Structure in American Life*, co-authored by Charles Murray and the late Richard J. Herrnstein (Herrnstein and Murray, 1994), a work which rapidly became one of the most controversial and headline-grabbing contributions to the debate about 'race', class and intelligence. In this book, the authors reiterated many of Arthur Jensen's earlier claims, maintaining that there was an enormous amount of very credible evidence showing that the mean IQ of Asian Americans (referring principally to those from China and Japan) was a little higher than that of European Americans which was, in turn, considerably higher than that of African Americans. Much of the explanation for this phenomenon apparently lay in genetic rather than environmental factors.

Right at the outset, Herrnstein and Murray acknowledged that the principal themes of their book were capable of provoking considerable anxiety and disquiet:

> This book is about differences in intellectual capacity among people and groups and about what those differences mean for America's future. The relationships we will be discussing are among the most sensitive in contemporary America – so sensitive that hardly anyone writes or talks about them in public. . . . It is clear that people have shied away from the topic for many reasons. Some think that the concept of intelligence has been proved a fraud. Others recall totalitarian eugenic schemes based on IQ scores, or worry about such schemes arising once the subject breaks into the open. Many fear that discussing intelligence will promote racism. (p. xxi)

In the view of the authors, the situation that rendered publication of the book so necessary centred on the fragmentation and polarization of American society, with the rich and successful enjoying lives of affluence and fulfilment at the top of society and the poor and dispossessed enduring lives of misery at the bottom. A large proportion of the population belonged to neither group; but their lives were increasingly shaped by 'the power of the fortunate few and the plight of the despairing few'. According to Herrnstein and Murray, social scientists, journalists and politicians were seeking explanations for this state of affairs in all the wrong places:

> They examine changes in the economy, changes in demographics, changes in the culture. They propose solutions founded on better education, on more and better jobs, on specific social interventions. But they ignore an underlying element that has shaped the changes: human intelligence – the way it varies within the American population and its crucially changing role in our destinies during the last half of the twentieth century. To try to come to grips with the nation's problems without understanding the role of intelligence is to see through a glass darkly indeed, to grope with symptoms instead of causes, to stumble into supposed remedies that have no chance of working. (p. xxiii)

For Herrnstein and Murray, reform of the education system was one of the 'supposed remedies' that had 'no chance of working'. In the authors' view, the system served chiefly to reflect and indeed *intensify* existing divisions within society. We simply had to accept a situation where East Asians and European Americans consistently out-performed African Americans. We also had to accept the 'twin realities' that 'people differ in intelligence for reasons that are not their fault, and that intelligence has a powerful bearing on how well people do in life' (p. 527). There was obviously no point in providing additional resources for the education of the poor in a vain attempt to remedy a situation that was 'genetically determined'. Indeed, it was necessary for the Federal Government to shift money away from programmes for the disadvantaged to programmes for the gifted and highly intelligent. And it was also time for society to rediscover education's 'true purpose':

> Until the latter half of this century, it was taken for granted that the chief purpose of education was to educate the gifted – not

because they deserved it through their own merit, but because, for better or worse, the future of society was so dependent on them. It was further understood that this education must aim for more than mere technical facility. It must be an education that fosters wisdom and virtue through the ideal of the 'educated man'. Little will change until educators once again embrace this aspect of their vocation. (p. 418)

Having offered little by way of practical solutions to society's ills, the authors outlined a truly frightening vision of the future in the penultimate chapter of their book entitled 'The Way We Are Headed'. They accepted that 'predicting the course of society is chancy'; but there were certain future trends they considered 'inevitable and unavoidable'. They expected 'cognitive stratification' – the allocation of people to specific groups according to their cognitive ability – to lead to an increasingly isolated cognitive elite, a merging of the cognitive elite with the affluent, and a steadily deteriorating quality of life for those people 'at the bottom end of the cognitive ability distribution'. These trends would lead the US towards something resembling 'a caste society', with the 'underclass mired ever more firmly at the bottom, and the cognitive elite ever more firmly anchored at the top', able to 'restructure the rules of society' so that it became 'harder and harder for them to lose' (p. 509). In such a harsh meritocracy, racial tensions were bound to increase, hostilities become overt with a substantial part of the population reduced to living in modern versions of the Indian reservation. At the very least, it would become harder than ever before for people of 'low cognitive ability' to lead 'meaningful and dignified lives'.

Having downgraded the 'intellectually weak', Herrnstein and Murray ended their book by seeking ways of living with them. The way forward for the authors, outlined in their last chapter, 'A Place for Everyone', involved accepting society *as it was*, without making any attempt to radically change it. There should indeed be a *valued place* for everyone in society; but that had nothing to do with the pursuit of something called 'equality'. The concept of equality was a chimera, since nothing could be done to halt the process of 'cognitive partitioning':

Inequality of endowments, including intelligence, is a reality. Trying to pretend that inequality does not really exist has already led to disaster. Trying to eradicate inequality with artificially manufactured outcomes has also led to disaster. It is time for America once again to try living with inequality, *as life is lived*: understanding that each human being has strengths and weaknesses, qualities we admire and qualities we do not admire, competences and incompetences, assets and debits; that the success of each human life is not measured externally but internally; that of all the rewards we can confer on each other, the most precious is a place in society as a valued fellow citizen. (pp. 551–2)

When extracts from *The Bell Curve* appeared in the American magazine *The New Republic*, edited by Andrew Sullivan, it was felt necessary to accompany Murray's 11,000-word text with criticisms and responses in order to demonstrate the variety of strongly held opinions on the delicate matter of intelligence and 'race'. In a symposium specially put together by the Editor, a number of irate contributors denounced Murray's ideas as blatantly 'racist', using terms like 'racist chic' and 'newspeak about racial inferiority'. Many found the book reminiscent of the work of Hans Eysenck, who always maintained that Negroes and the Irish were intellectually inferior to the English, and of William Shockley, the Nobel prize-winning physicist who advocated sterilization for people with low IQs and sperm banks for geniuses (see Sullivan, 1994).

It is interesting to note that, in defending the work of Cyril Burt and Arthur Jensen, Herrnstein and Murray were very critical of rival views of intelligence, and, in particular, of the theory of 'multiple intelligences' advanced by Harvard psychologist Howard Gardner in his 1983 book *Frames of Mind* (Gardner, 1983). Rejecting the notion of a general intelligence factor, often known simply as 'g', Gardner argued the case for *seven* distinct 'intelligences' combinable in a variety of ways to form the intellectual repertoire of all human beings. Two of these, logical-mathematical intelligence and linguistic intelligence, were the attributes that IQ tests already focused on. The remaining 'intelligences' in Gardner's list comprised: the musical, the spatial, the bodily-kinaesthetic and two forms of 'personal intelligence', the intrapersonal and the interpersonal.

Gardner accepted that his approach to the subject of human ability was distinctly novel and unusual in that he made no attempt to back up his theory with quantitative data. In a field that had been intensely quantitative since its inception, his particular contribution was uniquely devoid of psychometric or other quantitative evidence. At the same time, he rejected the criticism that he had merely redefined the term 'intelligence' by broadening it to include what should more properly be called 'talents': 'I place no particular premium on the word *intelligence*', he wrote in 1983, 'but I do place great importance on the equivalence of various human faculties. If critics of my theory are willing to label language and logical thinking as talents as well, and to remove these from the pedestal they currently occupy, then I will be happy to speak in terms of *multiple talents*' (Gardner, 1983, p. xi). Without abandoning his basic approach, he later added to his original seven 'intelligences' both the classificatory intelligence of the naturalist and – although he had reservations about according this the status of a discrete intelligence – spiritual intelligence. He was fond of claiming, half-seriously, that while Socrates had viewed human beings as rational animals, he himself saw them as animals possessing 'eight-and-a-half intelligences'.

It is, of course, possible to criticize Gardner for the particular way in which he constructed his 'charmed circle of intelligences' (see, for example, White, 1998); but there is no doubt that his view of intelligence or ability as not being tied to IQ-tested skills has had a liberating effect on those children, often from deprived backgrounds invariably encouraged to think of themselves as 'dim' or 'slow-witted'. Thousands of so-called 'MI schools' have sprung up in recent years in America, Canada, Australia and elsewhere, all based on Gardner's theory. Some of Gardner's more ardent disciples, particularly in parts of Australia, actually believe that the entire school curriculum should be based on the development of his nine 'intelligences'. MI theory has also acted as a powerful liberating force in school improvement projects across Britain, from Birmingham and Sandwell in the West Midlands to Govan in Scotland. In the circumstances, it is hardly surprising that Herrnstein and Murray should have found Gardner's work both radical and threatening.

In the past ten years, some commentators in America have expressed surprise at the interest aroused by publication of *The Bell Curve*, as if eugenic ideas had somehow gone away in the 1970s and 1980s and were now making an unwelcome reappearance. Steven Selden, on the other hand, writing as an academic with many years' experience of investigating the influence of eugenic ideas on education in America, views this as a total misreading of the historical situation. In his book *Inheriting Shame: the Story of Eugenics and Racism in America*, published in 1999 (Selden, 1999), Professor Selden argued that it was surely testament to America's loss of collective memory that so many people were apparently surprised by the reassertion of genetically reductive approaches to complex social and educational issues. In Selden's view, eugenic theories had occupied a privileged place at the heart of social and educational policies and practices in America for much of the twentieth century. Indeed, the assumption of genetic reductivism had been one of the guiding principles not only of overtly right-wing movements, but also of 'progressive' educational and social tendencies as well. Educators of a wide range of political views had allowed themselves to be 'persuaded' by the leading advocates of eugenic thinking that, according to the latest scientific 'evidence', all manner of human moral, intellectual and social characteristics could be 'explained' by heredity. Even the major biology and social studies textbooks in use in most schools in the USA simply accepted eugenic ideas as 'common sense'. So it can be argued that popular eugenic theories actually *acquired* their popularity through the official knowledge sponsored by the state. And the 'return' of genetically reductive arguments to the arena of policy debates following the publication of *The Bell Curve* was not really in any sense a return. Eugenic ideas had never, in fact, gone away: they were always there, embodied in the constant struggles over sufficient funding for the education of the poor and for a school system that was less elitist and less classed, raced and gendered.

New Labour and Concepts of Ability

Eugenic ideas have also enjoyed a long life in Britain; though government ministers would probably be slow to recognize the eugenic origins of some of the ideas on 'ability' and 'intelligence' expressed in government documents, White Papers and ministerial speeches.

The first education White Paper of the New Labour Government was published by the Department for Education and Employment in July 1997, just 67 days after Tony Blair's remarkably decisive victory in the May General Election. This 84-page document with the title *Excellence in Schools* contained a Foreword by the new Secretary of State David Blunkett emphasizing the importance of rejecting excuses for 'under-performance' in schools:

> To overcome economic and social disadvantage and to make
> equality of opportunity a reality, we must strive to eliminate, and

never excuse, under-achievement in the most deprived parts of our country. Educational attainment encourages aspiration and self-belief in the next generation; and it is through family learning, as well as scholarship through formal schooling, that success will come. . . . We must overcome the spiral of disadvantage, in which alienation from, or failure within, the education system is passed from one generation to the next. (DfEE, 1997, p. 3)

The White Paper asserted, though without supporting evidence, that mixed ability teaching had proved successful 'only in the hands of the best teachers' and should be used in future only where 'there was proof that it could be truly effective'. Chapter 4, with the title 'Modernizing the Comprehensive Principle', argued that, while there could be no return to the days of eleven-plus selection, there was a clear need to 'reform' and 'modernize' the comprehensive school to take account of evolving needs.

We are not going back to the days of the old eleven-plus; but neither are we prepared to stand still and defend the failings of across-the-board mixed ability teaching. The debate over grouping approaches is sterile and provides no solutions. We intend to modernize comprehensive education to create inclusive schooling which provides a broad, flexible and motivating education that recognizes the different talents of all children and delivers excellence for everyone. (ibid., p. 37)

The document made a presumption that 'setting should be the norm in secondary schools', with primary schools also considering its use with older pupils. The challenge for teachers at all levels was to ensure that all children, whatever their talents, developed their diverse abilities:

We believe in 'diversity within one campus', with the method of teaching and the organization of a school playing to the strengths of every child. Mixed ability grouping has not proved capable of doing this in all schools. It requires excellent teaching, and while it has sometimes worked well, in too many cases, it has failed *both* to stretch the brightest *and* to respond to the needs of those who have fallen behind. Setting, particularly in science, maths and languages, is proving effective in many schools. We do not believe that any single model of grouping pupils should be *imposed* on secondary schools, but unless a school can clearly demonstrate that it is getting better than expected results through a different approach, we do make the presumption that setting should be the norm in secondary schools. In some cases, and with some pupils, it is worth considering in primary schools. Schools should make clear in their reports to parents the use they are making of different grouping approaches. OFSTED inspections will also report on this. (ibid., p. 38)

The White Paper further announced that the Government planned to develop a strategy for 'the early identification and support of particularly able and talented children' that linked several elements, including: 'accelerated learning for some pupils, specialist schools and partnership with independent schools' (ibid., p. 39).

Successive government documents issued between 1997 and 2005 continued to prioritize the 'needs' of the able and talented. For example: the *Five Year Strategy for Children and Learners*, presented to Parliament by Education Secretary Charles Clarke in July 2004, contained a section on 'gifted and talented students' which made specific reference to the National Academy for Gifted and Talented Youth (NAGTY) established in 2002. In the words of the 2004 document:

The Government will . . . give extra support to pupils who have not been well-served by the education system in the past, including gifted and talented students. . . . Many schools lack the confidence to attend fully to the needs of able pupils and ensure that they achieve their highest potential. The new National Academy for Gifted and Talented Youth (NAGTY) is intended to be a centre of excellence advising teachers on the best way to teach gifted young people, and to encourage them to go on to university, offering summer schools and on-line learning for gifted and talented young people, so that they can meet and work with other like-minded children and be given extra stretch and challenge. (DfES, 2004, p. 60)

There was also reference to the National Academy in the section on 'gifted and talented learners' in the White Paper *Higher Standards, Better Schools for All*, published in October 2005. This White Paper also included a proposal of which Francis Galton would have heartily approved: the setting up of a national register of 'gifted and talented pupils', although there was at least an acknowl-edgement in the document that such pupils did not necessarily always come from the upper and middle classes:

> A tailored education means addressing the needs of the most gifted and talented, just as much as those who are struggling. These children will come from every background – children from disadvantaged backgrounds are just as likely to be gifted and talented as those from the middle class, and may need greater support to fulfil their potential. . . . We will . . . work with secondary schools to ensure that they are identifying all their gifted and talented pupils. Using schools' identifications, alongside data on pupils' performance at the end of Key Stage 2 and other widely used tests of ability, we will develop a national register of gifted and talented pupils. This will allow us to invite all who fall within the top 5 per cent to join NAGTY, so that they can benefit fully from the opportunities offered through its student academy. We will also use the register to help provide the right local opportunities to extend gifted and talented pupils' studies, and to support pupils' progression into higher education. . . . NAGTY has provided residential summer schools for up to 1,000 gifted and talented pupils each year since 2002. We have now asked NAGTY, working with the Specialist Schools and Academies Trust, to develop a national programme of non-residential summer schools, to run alongside the summer schools for gifted and talented pupils that individual local authorities and schools are already providing. We will seek private sponsorship for these new summer schools. (DfES, 2005, pp. 55–6)[1]

And this 2005 White Paper included a quite extraordinary statement emphasizing (rightly) that all pupils must be encouraged to reach 'the limits of their capacity', while, at the same time, dividing children into three main categories: 'the gifted and talented, the struggling and the just average' (ibid., p. 20).

The obsession with the 'needs' of so-called gifted and talented children, so evident in *The Bell Curve* and New Labour White Papers, was something that particularly troubled the late Caroline Benn, who argued that comprehensive schooling was primarily concerned with developing the abilities and talents that *all* children possessed (see Benn and Chitty, 2004). She well understood that even though terms like 'intelligent', 'backward', 'more able', 'average' and 'less able' were not often spoken in their hearing, young people soon appreciated the nature of the category to which they had been allocated by teachers and others and where they and their friends fitted into the pernicious hierarchy of ability. In her view, even the term 'mixed-ability teaching' was flawed in that it did not necessarily imply a radical break with ill-conceived notions of 'fixed ability'. She had developed her ideas in two articles written for the journal *Forum* in 1982 (Benn, 1982a and 1982b) in which she set out to challenge what she called 'the myth of giftedness' and to argue for the encouragement of human ability in all its various forms:

> We give up our commitment to looking for gifts, talents and abilities in the vast majority of children once we have accepted the argument that the search for 'giftedness' is limited to the hunt for a few. . . . The way we can support 'giftedness' (whatever it may mean) is by encouraging a flexible, alert, high-standard, stimulating and supportive comprehensive education service for everyone at every stage of their lives. . . . A comprehensive system is the only way we can openly ensure attention to all equally and, at the same time, protect and reveal the full range of human gifts. Encouraging human ability in all its various forms is just one more reason why we must continue to work to get a genuine comprehensive education system safely started in Britain – and to promote it relentlessly when we have. (Benn, 1982b, p. 84)

In areas outside education as such, and tackling the broader problems of crime and social exclusion, Prime Minister Tony Blair has recently voiced opinions that have been criticized for toying with ideas commonly associated with 'genetic determinism'. In a well-publicized speech on social exclusion, delivered on 31 August 2006, the Prime Minister argued that tomorrow's potential troublemakers could sometimes be identified, even before they were born. Tony Blair said it was often possible to spot the families whose circumstances made it likely that their children would have mental or behavioural problems, indulge in anti-social behaviour and generally be 'a menace to society'. In his opinion, there had to be effective intervention, 'pre-birth even'. He made it clear that he was not talking about the state interfering with 'normal family life', but that he was referring specifically to those families that could be labelled as 'dysfunctional':

I am saying that where it is clear, as it very often is, at a very young age, that some children are at risk of being brought up in a dysfunctional home where there are multiple problems, say of drug abuse or offending, then instead of waiting until the child goes off the rails, we should act early enough, with the right help, support and disciplined framework for the family, to prevent it. This is not stigmatizing the child or the family. It may indeed be the only way to save them and the wider community from the consequences of inaction. . . . Extra financial help, at least on its own, is not what is needed. What *is* needed . . . is proper structured help – and at a stage early enough to make a difference. . . . And it is not as if there is no evidence base on which to draw. The truth is that around the world, in societies similar to our own, all forms of social exclusion are common. There is now a wealth of empirical data to analyse. And the purport of it is clear. You can detect and predict the children and families likely to go wrong. The vast majority offered help take it. And early intervention is far more effective than the colossal expenditure of effort and resources once things have gone wrong. This is the lesson from Europe, the USA, New Zealand and many other countries. (Blair, 2006)

Among the main solutions and ways forward offered in the Speech was that social workers should intervene much earlier to prevent the children in 'dysfunctional' families turning into 'problem teenagers'. And families who refused to cooperate could lose their state benefits or have their children taken into local authority care more swiftly. The new approach would involve 'complex and variegated decision-making'. Agencies needed incentives to cooperate more closely with one another. It was necessary 'to liberate professionals to work ingeniously and strip away the rules, conventions and hierarchies that prevented them doing what was best in each individual case'.

This Speech aroused a good deal of controversy and criticism. Anastasia de Waal, Head of the Family and Education Unit at the think-tank Civitas, said: 'It is surely teetering on genetic determinism to go in for this kind of saying that before some children are even born, they can be labelled as "problematic"' (reported in the *Independent*, 1 September 2006). And Norman Lamb, Chief of Staff to Liberal Democrat Leader Sir Menzies Campbell, commented: 'Empty threats to pregnant mothers will do little to restore confidence in a government that has failed to tackle poverty, crime and social exclusion for the last nine years' (ibid).[2]

On 21 November 2006, the Government followed up Tony Blair's Speech on social exclusion by announcing plans for 'supporting' parents in need with 'parenting classes' designed to halt the spread of juvenile delinquency. In an initiative covering 77 local council areas in England and Wales, harassed parents could volunteer to participate in one or other of the taxpayer-funded schemes; but those whose children consistently misbehaved or played truant from school could be forced to attend a twelve-week programme to be 'advised' on how to bring them up. If they refused to attend, they could be fined; but the Home Office said it was confident that, in the vast majority of cases, sanctions would not prove necessary (reported in the *Daily Telegraph*, 22 November 2006).

Issues of 'race' and multiculturalism have also featured prominently in reports and stories in the national media in Britain. We saw in Chapter 6 that in the 1960s, a number of local authorities adopted a policy borrowed from America whereby a minority of black children were 'bussed' into predominantly white areas to prevent the creation in large cities of all-black 'sink' schools. And concern still exists that in some of Britain's cities, non-white pupils form 90 per cent of the population of one secondary school, while white pupils constitute 90 per cent of a neighbouring school just down the road. In a front-page story headed 'Race quotas needed to end divide in schools', published on 12 October 2006, *The Times* gave details of an interview it had conducted with Lord Bruce-Lockhart, Head of the Local Government Association, in which he argued that 'state schools should introduce ethnic quotas into admissions criteria to break down the extreme segregation of pupils along cultural and religious lines'. In Lord Bruce-Lockhart's view, Britain would never achieve integration and full social cohesion while neighbouring schools were divided along 'ethnic lines'. While reluctant to specify a quota, the former Conservative Leader of Kent County Council suggested it would probably have to be set at around 25 per cent. All of which may sound very reasonable; but critics of the proposal have pointed out that ethnic quotas have been shown to be unworkable in the US, where the problem of pupil segregation is far more extreme. And all such proposals contain implicit assumptions about 'race' and ability which continue to go unchallenged in large sections of the media.

Conclusion: Prospects for the Future

It would be wrong to give the impression that the idea of fixed innate ability has not been challenged in both Britain and America. Indeed, academics and teachers in both countries have provided detailed and challenging critiques of the practices of ability labelling and ability-focused teaching based on determinist beliefs about ability and intelligence.

The Idea of Learning without Limits

One very important research project designed to explore ways of teaching and learning free from these determinist beliefs about so-called ability was the Learning without Limits Project set up at the University of Cambridge School of Education in 1999; and discussion of the findings of this significant piece of research, written up in *Learning without Limits* published in 2004 (Hart, Dixon, Drummond and McIntyre, 2004), provides us with the opportunity to conclude this book on a note of optimism and hope. The book was dedicated to the late Brian Simon (1915–2002), whose pioneering work on the false assumptions of intelligence testing had profoundly influenced the thinking of all those participating in the enterprise; and the actual name of the Project was inspired by the following powerful passage from Stephen Jay Gould's *The Mismeasure of Man* which seemed to capture the authors' central concerns:

> We pass through this world but once. Few tragedies can be more extensive than the stunting of life, few injustices deeper than the denial of an opportunity to strive or even to hope, by a limit imposed from without, but falsely identified as lying within. (Gould, 1981, pp. 28–9)

The key idea of the Project was to bring together a group of experienced classroom teachers who had rejected ideas of fixed innate ability and to study their practice in order to try to identify the chief concepts and methods that could be said to be distinctive of teaching free from preconceived assumptions about ability and intellectual development.

In the view of the project leaders, too many classroom teachers throughout the twentieth century used the concept of ability as 'a natural way of talking about children'. Even when they consciously rejected the idea that 'potential' was permanently fixed, they often felt comfortable in using ability labels to refer to differences in young people's *current* abilities to *do* certain things. This essentially 'performance' view of achievement certainly allowed for a much more sophisticated and nuanced view of individual abilities. Any particular pupil might, in theory, be among the 'most able' in some subjects and among the 'least able' in others. In practice, however, it often transpired that the same child came to be seen as either 'more able' or 'less able' in most areas of the curriculum, or at least in the 'high-status' academic subjects. In the absence of an alternative explanation, there was a temptation to infer from these recurring patterns that obvious differences in attainment did indeed reflect immutable differences in underlying general cognitive ability.

At the secondary level, there was a special emphasis on the need for teachers to differentiate their teaching adequately to cater for the specific requirements of students at different points on the ability spectrum. This was a point highlighted in HMI and Ofsted reports in the 1990s, particularly in relation to teaching in 'mixed ability' classes. In the event, this official endorsement of 'differentiation by ability' often led to the rationing of opportunity and resources, rather than having the effect of enhancing achievement for all. In research carried out in two secondary schools, David Gillborn and Deborah Youdell found that because the performance tables based on GCSE results concentrated on the percentage of sixteen-year-old students in each school achieving the 'top' A* to C grades, there was enormous pressure on teachers to concentrate all their efforts on their 'average' students, while neglecting those unfortunate youngsters thought incapable of gaining at least five of those all-important A* to C grades. In other words, secondary schools were finding it necessary to 'ration' their attention and efforts in order to concentrate on those students at the 'borderline' between grades C and D (see Gillborn and Youdell, 1999; 2000).

In putting forward a new and liberating concept of teaching and learning, the nine classroom teachers chosen to participate in the Learning without Limits Project made it clear that the key to human intellectual development was not *heredity* but *education*. The alternative kind of learning endorsed in their individual accounts was learning that was, in the words of the 2004 book:

> free from the needless constraints imposed by ability-focused practices, free from the indignity of being labelled top, middle or bottom, fast or slow, free from the wounding consciousness of being treated as someone who can aspire at best to only limited achievements. (Hart, Dixon, Drummond and McIntyre, 2004, p. 3)

No longer was there any promotion by the teacher of the self-fulfilling prophecy, described by Rosenthal and Jacobson in their famous 1968 study *Pygmalion in the Classroom* (Rosenthal and Jacobson, 1968), whereby pupils tended to live up to or down to what they believed was *expected* of them. The kind of learning supported by the nine teachers accepted that explaining differences in terms of inherent and fixed ability was not only unjust and untenable, but also deprived classroom teachers of the chance to 'base and develop their practice upon a more complex, multifaceted and infinitely more empowering understanding of teaching and learning processes and of all the influences, internal and external to the school, that impinged on learning and achievement' (ibid., p. 17).

In their 2004 book, Susan Hart and her colleagues pointed out that echoes of the model of pedagogy promoted by the nine teachers were certainly present in the work of Brian Simon who argued as long ago as 1953 (Simon, 1953) that all teachers should start out from the conviction that *all* the children under their care were *educable*. He also believed strongly that the classroom teacher should begin by focusing on the interests that the pupils shared, rather than by emphasizing and promoting their individual differences. In Brian Simon's words:

> The teacher who sets out to *educate* the children under his [*sic*] care, meets them as human beings. He first searches for ways of welding his class together into a group, knowing that learning is not a purely individual affair which takes place in a vacuum, but rather a *social activity*; and that the progress of each child will be conditioned largely by the progress of the group *as a*

whole. He begins, then, by concentrating on the interests children have in common, rather than by underlining their individual differences. As the work of the class takes shape, however, individual children make varying contributions: some may draw well, other may be good readers, others may be quick with figures. The teacher's task is not, of course, to see that the children who are good at some particular activity shine *to the detriment of their companions,* but rather to see that each child contributes to and enlivens the work of the class as a whole, and that all encompass the necessary basic skills. There is surely no better means of ensuring this than the stimulus given by other children within a cohesive group. (Simon, 1953, p. 103)

Brian Simon believed that the teachers who approached their task in this way started out from a point of view 'diametrically opposed to the philosophy underpinning mental testing'. Their attitude was 'essentially humanist'. They recognized that learning was 'a process of human change, not merely the formal acquisition of knowledge' (ibid.). This did not, of course, mean that teachers committed to the idea of human educability simply shut their eyes to obvious differences in attainment. What it *did* mean was that they refused to be blinded by the assumption that degrees of attainment somehow reflected immutable degrees of 'intelligence'. The teacher's role was to develop and shape abilities and talents in an optimistic and open-ended way. All teachers had to be specifically skilled at this extremely complex and important task and to set about it in a systematic manner. To do precisely this was indeed the essence of education. It followed that the degree to which teachers were successful in their work depended to a considerable extent on their attitude to the job, which was, in turn, coloured by their attitude to children. In Simon's words:

If, led astray by the theories of mental testing, the teacher believes that the level of a child's achievement is *predetermined* by the nature of his inborn 'abilities', then all he can aim to do is to help children to make their inborn 'abilities' *actual.* He does not conceive that a child can rise above his inheritance. From the start, therefore, he does not set out to educate *in a creative way.* . . . If, on the other hand, the teacher believes that the development of a child's abilities depends primarily on the careful control of the child's activity in school, that is on the nature and character of his own teaching, then his attitude will be entirely different. In this case, he holds that it is possible to *educate* the child in the fullest sense of the term, and he will exert his skill and his art precisely to assist him constantly to rise above himself, to make ever new achievements, and to overcome all obstacles in his path. (ibid., p. 105)

Current Government Policy and the Future

There is, of course, no evidence that the New Labour Government, regardless of the views of the particular individuals who constitute the Cabinet, is prepared to contemplate a departure from an obsession with ability labelling and ability-focused teaching. As we saw in the last chapter, the 2005 education White Paper *Higher Standards, Better Schools for All* allocated pupils to one or other of three distinct groups: 'the gifted and talented, the struggling and the just average' (DfES, 2005, p. 20). And talk about the need for special treatment for the 'gifted' and the 'talented' (which seems on the surface to be totally unproblematic) is often little more than a subtle way of legitimizing the process of academic selection, a point made by the late Caroline Benn in the first of her two *Forum* articles on 'The myth of giftedness', published in the Spring of 1982:

> The gifted child is indeed a very difficult concept to challenge, since it already enjoys a fine public image (one reason it has been misused so easily) and because most of us accept willingly that some children are possessed of extraordinary talent. It is only when we look behind the scenes that we see quite clearly the way 'giftedness' has taken the place of the old 'ability at eleven' as the justification for continuing with some form of academic selection. (Benn, 1982a, p. 51)

At the same time, the Conservative Opposition led by David Cameron recommends a rigid adherence to forms of streaming and/or setting at the secondary level as a way of compensating for what it sees as one of the least desirable assumptions of comprehensive schooling, namely: the idea that children of different 'abilities' can be educated together. All of which seems to give little cause for optimism.

Yet if we continue with our policy of looking for evidence of progress and enlightenment, it is important to stress that many classroom teachers do *not* believe that ability is either fixed or innate. *Learning without Limits* was very well received by critics, one reviewer, Professor Tim Brighouse (Brighouse, 2004), stating at the very outset of his piece in *The Times Educational Supplement* that 'here is a book that could change the world'. In Brighouse's view:

> A growing number of teachers, including the nine in this book, passionately believe in the limitless potential of the youngsters they teach. Of course, they care about their pupils, but they also care (with a sincerity that communicates itself to these pupils) about the pupils *they might become*, and are never resigned to them achieving less than their potential. (ibid.)

Professor Brighouse went on to list what he saw as the qualities of successful teachers:

> They build confidence and emotional security; they strengthen feelings of competence and control; they increase enjoyment and purposefulness; they honour and enhance pupils' identities as learners; they increase hope and confidence in their pupils' fortunes; they help the individual to know his or her role as part of a community – and in doing all that, they can provide access for all young people to knowledge, understanding and skills of significance to the learner's future. Finally, they increase relevance, reveal meaning and enable thinking, reasoning and explanations. (ibid.)

In an article published in *The Times Educational Supplement* in June 2004, one of the book's authors, Mary Jane Drummond (Drummond, 2004) hoped that the book would:

> convince the Government of the need to replace their current policies with an improvement agenda committed to freeing education from the damaging effects of the fixed-ability mind-set. (ibid.)

She went on:

> School improvement need not be dependent upon schools being put under constant pressure, bombarded by a succession of externally-imposed initiatives. In the Learning without Limits

model, the drive to improve things, to keep looking for ways to increase and enhance everybody's learning capacity is inscribed in the very nature of teaching. (ibid.)

If only education ministers could find the time to read *Learning without Limits*, and texts with a similar message, they might view their task very differently.

No longer would it be the purpose of schooling to allocate children to particular groups, each with a specific ability label attached to it. We need to (re)discover a belief in human educability, which was, after all, the original basis for the comprehensive reform. It is only when we dismantle all the structures rooted in the fallacy of fixed ability or potential that we will have a truly effective state education system.

Notes

Notes for Chapter 1

1. The term 'voluntaryism' was used by nineteenth-century writers to describe a mode of educational development free of state control and based on the independent initiative and financial resources of private individuals and organizations and on the voluntary attendance of children.
2. The work of the London School Board was phased out in 1903–4, following the passing of the 1902 Education Act which abolished all School Boards.
3. Sherlock Holmes made these observations to a somewhat incredulous Dr Watson as the Portsmouth train in which they were travelling approached Waterloo in 'The Adventure of the Naval Treaty', first published in *The Strand Magazine*, Vol. 6 (October–November 1893) and later included in *The Memoirs of Sherlock Holmes*.

Notes for Chapter 2

1. All four biographies have been able to make use of Francis Galton's own *Memories of my Life*, the first edition of which was published by Methuen in October 1908.
2. In the first volume of his Life of Francis Galton, Karl Pearson wrote that 'few men have had more noteworthy ancestry than Francis Galton' (Pearson, 1914, p. 60).
3. Charles Darwin himself formed a very high opinion of *Hereditary Genius*, as he made clear in a letter he wrote to Francis Galton on 3 December 1869: 'I have only read about fifty pages of your book, but already I can say I do not think I ever in all my life read anything more interesting and original – and how well and clearly you put every point! . . . You have made a

convert of an opponent in one sense, for I have always maintained that, excepting fools, men did not differ very much in intellect, only in zeal and hard work; and I still think this *may* be an eminently important point. Nevertheless, I congratulate you on producing what I am convinced will prove a memorable work.' On another occasion, Darwin wrote: 'I am now inclined to agree with Francis Galton in believing that education and environment produce only a small effect on the mind of anyone, and that most of our qualities are innate' (quoted in Gillham, 2001, pp. 155, 169).

4. Galton's new thinking is largely to be found in an article entitled 'Hereditary Improvement' published in 1873 in Volume 7 of *Fraser's Magazine.* Here he argued that his bold goal was 'to improve the race of man by a new system which shall be perfectly in accordance with the moral sense of the present time' (quoted in Gillham, 2001, p. 195).

5. Galton's father Tertius had purchased an estate at Claverdon, a village near Stratford-on-Avon in Warwickshire, in 1824, intending it to be used as a summer residence for all the family.

6. A full account of the proceedings of the First International Congress of Eugenics is to be found in Nicholas Gillham's Biography of Francis Galton, pp. 345–53.

7. Initially, only 'feebleminded' men were sterilized using vasectomy, but, by 1920, regular operations were being performed on women as well, using tubal ligation, which was by this time considered to be a relatively safe procedure.

8. In 1936, at the age of 76, Ploetz was actually appointed by Hitler to a professorship at Munich University. By this stage in his life, Ploetz was a radical anti-Semite and a fervent believer in the concept of Nordic supremacy (see Cornwell, 2003, pp. 78–80).

9. The SS (Schutz Staffel or Protection Squad) began life in a small way as Hitler's bodyguard. By the mid-1930s, SS troops had become the chief enforcers of Nazi discipline in the Nazi state. Under Heinrich Himmler, they ran the concentration camps and took responsibility for the extermination of the Jews.

Notes for Chapter 3

1. Even in Victorian England, large families had often been regarded by upper- and middle-class parents with more dismay

than satisfaction. Queen Victoria, who herself bore four sons and four daughters, found childbearing distinctly distasteful and large families unappealing. When the Princess of Wales produced her fourth child and Victoria's fourteenth grandchild in 1868, the Queen dismissed the event in a letter as 'very uninteresting – for all this seems to me to go on like the rabbits in Windsor Park!' (quoted in Read, 1979, p. 215).

2. The 'den of the sweater' refers to the 'sweat-shop', such as in the clothing industry in London's East End, where gangs of workers toiled in wretched conditions for very low wages.

3. Francis Wheen discusses the reasons for Wells's 1905 'retreat' from the extreme positions adopted in *Anticipations* in his Introduction to the 2005 Penguin edition of *A Modern Utopia*.

4. According to Friedrich Nietzsche (1844–1900), Zarathustra (or Zoroastres) was the founder of an ancient Persian religion, with its own Bible, the Zend-Avesta. He is said to have lived in the seventh century BC, though since the nineteenth century, many scholars have questioned whether he actually existed. At the heart of the religion is a conflict between Ahura Mazda (Ormuzd), the God of Light and Good and Angra Mainyu (Ahriman), the God of Darkness and Evil. It is interesting to note that the German composer Richard Strauss (1864–1949), whose own relationship with Hitler's Nazi Government was ambivalent to say the least, chose 'Also Sprach Zarathustra' as the title for one of his major works.

5. In *The Will to Power*, a work which consisted of a selection taken from Nietzsche's notebooks in the period from 1883 to 1888, Nietzsche wrote that: 'A declaration of war on the masses by *higher men* is now needed! Everywhere the mediocre are combining in order to give themselves mastery. . . . But the annihilation of the "decaying races" will create the possibility for the rearing of a new "master race" – the future "masters of the earth"' (pp. 458, 504).

6. The point is made by David Bradshaw in his Introduction to the 1994 Vintage Classics edition of *Brave New World*.

7. In the 1930s, Raymond B. Cattell was the education psychologist advising the Leicester Education Committee. He was also the author of a much-used *Guide to Mental Testing*, published in 1936.

8. *Ben Bulben* is a mountain north of Sligo.

9. *On the Boiler* was intended to be the first of a series of occasional publications. The title refers to an eccentric old

ship's carpenter that Yeats had heard about who used to utter denunciations to passers-by from an old boiler situated on the quay in Sligo.

10. Lord Nuffield (1877–1963) was a motor manufacturer and generous educational benefactor.

11. These points were made in the BBC Radio Four Programme 'Why Did We Do That? Eugenics', broadcast on 16 June 2003.

12. It is worth pointing out that it was not, in fact, uncommon for some people in Britain to approve of at least *some* of the policies that Hitler was implementing in Germany. In her published account of life in Barrow-in-Furness during the Second World War, housewife and mother Nella Last wrote in the entry in her diary for Sunday, 19 January 1941:

> I never thought I'd admire anything that Hitler did, but today, when I read in 'the Sunday Express' that he 'painlessly gassed' some thousands of lunatics, I did so. I believe firmly in euthanasia in incurable cases, whether of cancer, etc., or of mind disease. Far from being cruel, I think it's the reverse – and cruel in the extreme to *withhold* the 'gift of sleep'. If I ever get to the stage when I would be a burden or endless worry to anyone, I'd 'start off on my own'. Not in any spectacular way – just quietly, with the least possible fuss or bother – and count it no sin. I've often talked to nurses, and heard their views, and been surprised sometimes to find that they coincide with my own – that death should be brought to those who find life too hard to bear. I've heard so often the argument, 'Who is to judge?' or 'Who is to take responsibility?' But then, who is to condemn people to terrible pain – or the horror of incurable insanity and downright madness – and deny the draught that would set them free? I felt like an argument on the subject, and started off, but to my *intense* surprise, my husband agreed heartily, and went further. He said he thought every able-bodied nurse and doctor, and even 'ordinary people', will have enough to do to succour and bring to health the mentally fit, and that all food and services should be reserved for the sick and wounded (Broad and Fleming, 2006, pp. 95–6).

Notes for Chapter 4

1. Adrian Wooldridge has provided an enthusiastic account of Karl Pearson's work in the Eugenics Laboratory at University College, London, between 1911 and 1933 in his 1994 book *Measuring the Mind*. 'Endowed with ample research time, money and space, and inspired by an unshakeable commitment to biometry, the statistical study of evolution and heredity, Karl Pearson turned his Department into the focus of the English School of eugenic statistics, attracting researchers from the continent and the United States as well as Britain and pioneering a number of statistical breakthroughs' (Wooldridge, 1994, p. 78). In a speech delivered at his farewell dinner held at University College on 23 April 1934, Professor Pearson spoke admiringly of the eugenic experiments being conducted in Nazi Germany: 'The culmination of "biometrics" lay in Galton's preaching of eugenics and in his foundation of my Eugenics Professorship. But was this really the "culmination"? No, that lies rather in the future, with Reichkanzler Hitler and his proposals to regenerate the German people. In Germany at present a vast experiment is in hand, and some of you may live to see its results. If it fails, and we must hope it does not, it will not be for the want of enthusiasm, but rather because the Germans are only just embarking on the systematic study of mathematical statistics in the modern sense' (from Speeches delivered at a dinner held in University College, London, in honour of Professor Karl Pearson, 23 April 1934, privately printed at the University Press, Cambridge, in 1934, and passed on to the author by the late Professor Brian Simon).

2. When Cyril Burt moved to University College, London, in 1932, his post with the London County Council was frozen, and a successor was not appointed until 1949.

3. Variations of this idea, albeit couched in less extreme terms, are still in vogue at the start of the twenty-first century. The New Labour Government launched a national register of 'gifted' and 'talented' children in July 2006. Initially, the Register would be confined to secondary-age pupils, but it would later be expanded to include all four to nineteen-year-olds identified as 'gifted' and 'talented' by their schools.

Notes for Chapter 5

1. Deborah Thom has pointed out (Thom, 2004, p. 524) that no copy of this pre-war intelligence test survives, although it was one that Brian Simon used on a number of occasions, including in an article published in *Communist Review* in October 1949 (Simon, 1949).
2. In his recently published book *Intelligence, Destiny and Education*, Professor John White argues persuasively that the eugenic vision, and particularly with regard to concepts of human intelligence, has its ideological roots in the more 'radical' forms of Protestantism which underpinned the puritan and dissenting communities of the seventeenth century and later, on both sides of the Atlantic. In John White's view, 'predestination is as much a key feature of intelligence testing as it has been of Calvinism and its various puritan offshoots. In both systems, where one will end up in life – or indeed *after* life – is wholly or largely fixed at birth, whether by God or by nature. There is no way a person destined for damnation can come to be "saved", just as there is no way a child of very low IQ can hope to become a doctor or a lawyer' (White, 2006, p. 2).
3. The 'Peterloo Massacre' was the name given to a famous incident which took place at St Peter's Field in Manchester in August 1819 when a crowd of some 50,000 – 60,000 people, assembled to agitate for, among other things, the reform of Parliament, were set upon by the local Yeomanry, as a result of which eleven people were killed and several hundred badly injured.
4. A total of five Black Papers were published between 1969 and 1977. They mounted a sustained attack on the associated concepts of enhanced access to higher education, comprehensive education, egalitarianism and 'progressive' teaching methods in primary and secondary schools.

Notes for Chapter 6

1. It is now commonly accepted that the term 'race' should usually be placed, as here, in quotation marks, since it does not mean what many people think it means and its use is, to say the least, problematic and misleading. Many sociologists now argue that the term 'race' is actually 'socially constructed', arising out of

the 'pseudo-scientific' doctrines of the nineteenth century, which were chiefly concerned to promote the idea that the 'white' races were generally superior to all other groups. In fact, 'race' is not a viable biological concept and lacks *scientific* validity as a way of categorizing people. According to Gaine and George (1999, p. 5), 'a useful working definition of "race" is that of "a group of people who may share some physical characteristic to which social importance is attached"'. According to this viewpoint, the important facet of 'race' is not the skin colour, facial features or type of hair people have, but the *social significance* which is usually placed upon these.

2. The novelist C. P. Snow is referred to here in relation to certain statements he had made in America early in 1969 on Jewish intellectual and artistic achievements, which he had attributed to 'genetic endowment'. He later accepted that these unfortunate comments seemed to lend support to Jensen's thesis; and he also said that he wished Jensen had been 'a little more careful' (see Simon, 1971, p. 245).

3. The reference here is to Enoch Powell, Conservative MP for Wolverhampton South West, who delivered his notorious 'Rivers of Blood' Speech in Birmingham in April 1968. He chose Birmingham with its large 'immigrant' population as the ideal scene to warn West Midlands Conservatives – and the nation – of the dangers that lay ahead because of 'uncontrolled Black immigration'. He spoke of 'a total transformation to which there is no parallel in a thousand years of English history'; and he shared his deep foreboding about the future of the nation: 'As I look ahead, I am filled with a deep foreboding. Like the Roman, I seem to see "the River Tiber foaming with much blood"' (see Grosvenor, 1997, p. 103; Phillips and Phillips, 1998, p. 245).

4. The debate about the ethnic composition of the nation's secondary schools is still a lively issue. On 11 October 2006, Lord Bruce-Lockhart, Head of the Local Government Association, gave an interview to *The Times*, in which he argued that state schools should introduce ethnic quotas in order to break down 'the extreme segregation of pupils along racial and religious lines'. This is discussed more fully in the Conclusion.

5. The Hillgate Group was formed in 1986 to argue for a radical reform of the British education system, ensuring a devolution of real power from local education authorities to individual

schools – and ultimately to parents. The Group comprised: Caroline Cox, Jessica Douglas-Home, John Marks, Lawrence Norcross and Roger Scruton. Its first pamphlet *Whose Schools? A Radical Manifesto* (Hillgate Group, 1986) was published in December 1986.

6.   A full account of these developments is given in Professor Hearnshaw's biography of Sir Cyril Burt (see Hearnshaw, 1979, pp. 235–61).

7.   Margaret Jay's findings were written up in an article published in *The Listener*, 20 March 1986 (Jay, 1986).

8.   This is an extract from the comments that Keith Joseph made on the BBC Programme, broadcast on 28 February 1983.

Notes for Chapter 7

1.   The new National Register of Gifted and Talented Children was actually launched in July 2006. According to Schools Minister Lord Adonis, the Register would be confined initially to secondary-age pupils, but it would be expanded later to include *all* 4-to-19 year-olds identified as 'gifted and talented' by their schools. It was estimated that about 200,000 secondary-school pupils were in the top 5 per cent of the school population, on the basis of the English and maths national tests they sat as 11-year-olds. The Government was, however, concerned that no more than half of these pupils were members of the National Academy for Gifted and Talented Youth, so Lord Adonis wrote to all secondary headteachers in July 2006 urging them to nominate their 'brightest pupils' for membership of the Academy. In the event, over 30 per cent of headteachers failed to do so; and, partly as a result of this opposition, at the end of 2006, all secondary schools were told to supply the names of the top 10 per cent of their pupils when they completed the January 2007 schools census. According to a front-page story headed 'Vouchers to help 800,000 brightest pupils', which appeared in the *Daily Telegraph* on 28 December 2006, these gifted and talented pupils identified by each school were to be given 'vouchers' or 'credits' to buy a range of additional courses designed to foster their special talents.

2.   It is interesting to note that eugenic ideas are still alive in France in 2007. The right-wing candidate Nicolas Sarkozy provoked widespread criticism for making some remarkably eugenic

statements during his 2007 campaign to win the Presidency of France. In a French philosophy magazine, he outlined the view that individuals were probably predisposed to molest children. 'What part is innate and what acquired? We must not close the door to all debate,' he said. He added: 'I'm inclined personally to think that you are born a paedophile; and the problem is that we don't know how to treat this pathology.' The Archbishop of Paris, Monsignor Andre Vingt-Trois, led the criticism of Mr Sarkozy's views in a speech delivered on 10 April 2007: 'What seems most serious to me is the idea that you can't change the course of destiny.' And Marie-George Buffet, a leading member of the Communist Party, said that Mr Sarkozy's remarks were 'extremely serious' and 'from another era'. She went on: 'It goes back on everything that has evolved through science in our society. . . . We have to recognize that every man and woman is free and not predestined, whereas Mr Sarkozy says that their whole life is already written in their genes and that there's nothing thay can do about it.' (reported in *The Guardian*, 11 April 2007).

References

References for Chapter 1

Aldrich, R. (1982) *An Introduction to the History of Education.* London: Hodder and Stoughton.

Armytage, W. H. G. (1964) *Four Hundred Years of English Education.* Cambridge: Cambridge University Press.

Bamford, T. W. (1967) *The Rise of the Public Schools: A Study of Boys' Public Boarding Schools in England and Wales from 1837 to the Present Day.* London: Thomas Nelson.

Chitty, C. (1992) 'The changing role of the state in education provision'. *History of Education*, 21, 1, March, 1–13.

—— (1997) 'Interview with Keith Joseph', in P. Ribbins and B. Sherratt (eds), *Radical Educational Policies and Conservative Secretaries of State.* London: Cassell, pp. 78–86.

Colley, L. (1993) 'From the great bran-tub of dissent'. *Independent on Sunday*, 14 March.

Fraser, W. R. (1963) *Education and Society in Modern France.* London: Routledge.

Green, A. (1990) *Education and State Formation: the Rise of Education Systems in England, France and the USA.* London: Macmillan Press.

Hill, C. (1993) *The English Bible and the Seventeenth-Century Revolution.* London, Allen Lane: the Penguin Press.

Hobsbawm, E. J. (1968) *Industry and Empire: An Economic History of Britain since 1750.* London: Weidenfeld and Nicolson.

Johnson, R. B. (ed.) (1925) *The Letters of Hannah More.* London: The Bodley Head.

Mandeville, B. (1970 edition) *The Fable of the Bees*, Harmondsworth: Penguin.

Ranson, S. (1984) 'Towards a tertiary tripartism: new codes of social control and the 17+', in P. Broadfoot (ed.), *Selection,*

Certification and Control: Social Issues in Educational Assessment. Lewes: Falmer Press, pp. 221–44.

Rubinstein, D. (1977) 'Socialization and the London School Board 1870–1914: aims, methods and public opinion', in P. McCann (ed.), *Popular Education and Socialization in the Nineteenth Century*. London: Methuen, pp. 231–64.

Scruton, R. (1980) *The Meaning of Conservatism*. London: Macmillan.

Simon, B. (1960) *The Two Nations and the Educational Structure, 1780–1870*. London: Lawrence and Wishart.

——— (1965) *Education and the Labour Movement, 1870–1920*. London: Lawrence and Wishart.

Simon, J. (1966) *Education and Society in Tudor England*. Cambridge: Cambridge University Press.

Wiener, M. J. (1981) *English Culture and the Decline of the Industrial Spirit, 1850–1980*. Cambridge: Cambridge University Press.

Young, H. (1989) *One of Us: A Biography of Margaret Thatcher*. London: Macmillan.

References for Chapter 2

Areschoug, J. (2005) 'Between compulsory schooling and sterilization: education for feebleminded children, 1925–1954'. *History of Education Researcher*, 75, May, 14–25.

Berry, A. (2003) 'Whenever you can, count'. *London Review of Books*, 4 December, 23–5.

Brookes, M. (2004) *Extreme Measures: The Dark Visions and Bright Ideas of Francis Galton*. London: Bloomsbury.

Chitty, C. (2004) 'Eugenic theories and concepts of ability', in M. Benn, and C. Chitty (eds), *A Tribute to Caroline Benn: Education and Democracy*. London: Continuum, pp. 76–96.

Cornwell, J. (2003) *Hitler's Scientists: Science, War and the Devil's Pact*. London: Penguin Books.

Darwin, C. (1859) *The Origin of Species*. London: John Murray.

Evans, R. J. (2005) *The Third Reich in Power, 1933–1939*. London: Allen Lane.

Forrest, D. W. (1974) *Francis Galton: The Life and Work of a Victorian Genius*. New York: Taplinger Publishing Company.

Galton, F. (1853) *Tropical South Africa*. London: John Murray.

——— (1855) *The Art of Travel*. London: John Murray.

—— (1865) 'Hereditary Talent and Character'. *Macmillan's Magazine*, June, pp. 157–66; August, pp. 318–27.

—— (1869) *Hereditary Genius: An Inquiry into its Laws and Consequences*. London: Macmillan.

—— (1883) *Inquiries into Human Faculty and its Development*. London: Macmillan.

Galton, F. (1908) *Memories of My Life*. London: Macmillan.

Gillham, N. W. (2001) *A Life of Sir Francis Galton: From African Exploration to the Birth of Eugenics*. Oxford: Oxford University Press.

Hobsbawn, E. (1975) *The Age of Capital, 1848–1875*. London: Weidenfeld and Nicolson.

Huxley, T. H. (1888) 'The struggle for existence'. *Fortnightly Review*, 28–43.

Kershaw, I. (1998) *Hitler 1889–1936: Hubris*. London: Penguin Books.

King, D. (1999) *In the Name of Liberalism: Illiberal Social Policy in the United States and Britain*. Oxford: Oxford University Press.

Pearson, K. (1914; 1924; 1930) *The Life, Letters and Labours of Francis Galton*, Vol. 1 (1914); Vol. 2 (1924); Vols 3A and 3B (1930). Cambridge: Cambridge University Press.

Read, D. (1979) *England 1868–1914: The Age of Urban Democracy*. London: Longman.

Rees, L. (2005) *Auschwitz: The Nazis and the 'Final Solution'*. London: BBC Books.

References for Chapter 3

Boulton, J. T. (ed.) (1979) *The Letters of D. H. Lawrence*. Vol. 1, 1901–1913. Cambridge: Cambridge University Press.

Briggs, A. (1959) *The Age of Improvement, 1783–1867*. London: Longman.

Broad, R. and Fleming, S. (eds) (2006) *Nella Last's War: The Second World War Diaries of Housewife, 49*: London: Profile Books.

Carey, J. (1992) *The Intellectuals and the Masses: Pride and Prejudice among the Literary Intelligentsia, 1880–1939*. London: Faber and Faber.

Eliot, T. S. (1920) *Poems*. New York: A. A. Knopf.

Gillham, N. W. (2001) *A Life of Sir Francis Galton: From African*

Exploration to the Birth of Eugenics. Oxford: Oxford University Press.

Huxley, A. (1932) *Brave New World*, with an introduction by David Bradshaw (1994). London: Vintage Classics.

Kershaw, I. (1998) *Hitler 1889–1936: Hubris*. London: Penguin Books.

King, D. (1999) *In the Name of Liberalism: Illiberal Social Policy in the United States and Britain*. Oxford: Oxford University Press.

Lawrence, D. H. (1928) *Lady Chatterley's Lover*, with an introduction by Richard Hoggart (1961). Harmondsworth: Penguin Books.

Matthews, T. D. (1994) *Censored*. London: Chatto and Windus.

Nietzsche, F. (1883–85) *Also Sprach Zarathustra (Thus Spake Zarathustra)*, translated and with an introduction by R. J. Hollingdale (1961). Harmondsworth: Penguin Books.

—— (1883–88) *The Will to Power*, translated and with a commentary by R. J. Hollingdale and W. Kaufmann (1968). New York: Vintage Books.

Pugh, M. (2005) *'Hurrah for the Blackshirts!' Fascists and Fascism in Britain between the Wars*. London: Jonathan Cape.

Read, D. (1979) *England 1868–1914: The Age of Urban Democracy*. London: Longman.

Stopes, M. (1918) *Married Love*. London: Putnam.

Wells, H. G. (1901) *Anticipations of the Reaction of Mechanical and Scientific Progress Upon Human Life and Thought*. New York: Dover Publications.

—— (1905a) *Kipps: The Story of a Simple Soul*. London: Penguin Books.

—— (1905b) *A Modern Utopia*. London: Penguin Books.

Yeats, W. B. (1939a) *Last Poems and Two Plays*. Dundrum: Cuala Press.

—— (1939b) *On the Boiler*, republished in B. Larrissy (1997), *W. B. Yeats: A Critical Edition of the Major Works*. Oxford: Oxford University Press, pp. 389–96.

References for Chapter 4

Adami, G. (1923) 'The true aristocracy'. *The Eugenics Review*, 14, 174–86.

Board of Education (1938) *Report of the Consultative Committee* on *Secondary Education, with Special Reference to Grammar Schools and Technical High Schools* (Spens Report). London: HMSO.

Brown, I. (1988) 'Who were the Eugenicists? A study of the formation of an early twentieth-century pressure group'. *History of Education*, 17 (4), 295–307.

Burt, C. (1909) 'Experimental tests of general intelligence'. *British Journal of Psychology*, 3, 94–177.

——— (1913) 'The inheritance of mental characters', *The Eugenics Review*, 4, 168–200.

——— (1933) *How the Mind Works*. London: Allen and Unwin.

——— (1943) 'The psychological implications of the Norwood Report'. *British Journal of Educational Psychology*, 13, 126–40.

——— (1950) 'Testing intelligence'. *The Listener*, 16 November.

——— (1952) 'Cyril Burt', in E. G. Boring, H. S. Langfeld, H. Werner and R. M. Yerkes (eds), *History of Psychology in Autobiography*, Vol. 4. Worcester, MA: Clark University.

Gould, S. J. (1981) *The Mismeasure of Man*. New York: Norton.

Harte, N. and North, J. (1978) *The World of UCL, 1828–2004*. London: University College London.

Hearnshaw, L. (1979) *Cyril Burt – Psychologist*. London: Hodder and Stoughton.

Ministry of Education (1947) *Organization of Secondary Education* (Circular 144). London: HMSO.

Norton, B. (1981) 'Psychologists and class', in C. Webster (ed.), *Biology, Medicine and Society, 1840–1940*. Cambridge: Cambridge University Press, pp. 289–314.

Royal Commission (1908) *Report on the Care and Control of the Feebleminded*. London: HMSO.

Simon, B. (1974) *The Politics of Educational Reform, 1920–1940*. London: Lawrence and Wishart.

SSEC (Secondary Schools Examinations Council) (1943) *Curriculum and Examinations in Secondary Schools* (Norwood Report). London: HMSO.

White, J. (2006) *Intelligence, Destiny and Education: The Ideological Roots of Intelligence Testing*. London: Routledge.

Wooldridge, A. (1994) *Measuring the Mind: Education and Psychology in England, c. 1860 – c. 1990*. Cambridge: Cambridge University Press.

References for Chapter 5

Boyson, R. (1969) 'The essential conditions for the success of a comprehensive school', in C. B. Cox and A. E. Dyson (eds), *Black Paper Two: The Crisis in Education*. London: Critical Quarterly Society, pp. 57–62.

Burt, C. (1959) 'The examination at eleven plus'. *British Journal of Educational Studies*, 7, 99–117.

——— (1969) 'The mental differences between children', in C. B. Cox and A. E. Dyson (eds), *Black Paper Two: The Crisis in Education*. London: Critical Quarterly Society, pp. 16–25.

Chitty, C. (1989) *Towards a New Education System: The Victory of the New Right?* Lewes: Falmer Press.

——— (2002) *Understanding Schools and Schooling*. London: RoutledgeFalmer.

Clegg, A. (1953) 'Some problems of administration in West Riding grammar schools'. *Researches and Studies*, Vol. 7. University of Leeds Institute of Education, January, 3–12.

Crook, D. (2002) 'Local authorities and comprehensivization in England and Wales, 1944–1974'. *Oxford Review of Education*, 28 (2) and (3), June and September, 247–60.

DES (Department of Education and Science) (1967) *Children and their Primary Schools* (2 Vols: the Plowden Report). London: HMSO.

Douglas, J. W. B. (1964) *The Home and the School: A Study of Ability and Attainment in the Primary School*. London: MacGibbon and Kee.

Eysenck, H. J. (1969) 'The rise of the mediocracy', in C. B. Cox and A. E. Dyson (eds), *Black Paper Two: The Crisis in Education*. London: the Critical Quarterly Society, pp. 34–40.

Floud, J. E., Halsey, A. H. and Martin, F. M. (1956) *Social Class and Educational Opportunity*. London: Heineman.

Glass, D. V. (ed.) (1954) *Social Mobility in Britain*. London: Routledge.

Gould, S. J. (1981) *The Mismeasure of Man*. New York: Norton.

Grant, L. (1994) 'Inside story'. *Guardian Weekend*, 22 October, pp. 37–46.

Hearnshaw, L. (1979) *Cyril Burt – Psychologist*. London: Hodder and Stoughton.

Heim, A. (1954) *The Appraisal of Intelligence*. London: Methuen.

Jackson, B. (1961) 'Notes from two primary schools'. *New Left Review*, 11, September-October, 4–8.

Jackson, B. and Marsden, D. (1962) *Education and the Working Class*. London: Routledge and Kegan Paul.

Kamin, L. J. (1974) *The Science and Politics of IQ*. New York: John Wiley and Sons.

Kerckhoff, A. C., Fogelman, K., Crook, D. and Reeder, D. (1996) *Going Comprehensive in England and Wales: A Study of Uneven Change*. London: Woburn Press.

Kogan, M. (1971) *The Politics of Education: Edward Boyle and Anthony Crosland in Conversation with Maurice Kogan*. Harmondsworth: Penguin.

Lynn, R. (1969) 'Comprehensives and equality', in C. B. Cox and A. E. Dyson (eds), *Black Paper Two: The Crisis in Education*. London: Critical Quarterly Society, pp. 34–40.

Mason, S. (1965) 'Leicestershire', in S. Maclure (ed.), *Comprehensive Planning*. London: Councils and Education Press, pp. 51–8.

Ministry of Education (1963) *Half Our Future* (the Newsom Report). London: HMSO.

Pedley, R. (1963) *The Comprehensive School*. Harmondsworth: Penguin.

Plummer, G. (2000) *Failing Working-Class Girls*. Stoke-on-Trent: Trentham Books.

Simon, B. (1949) 'The theory and practice of intelligence testing'. *Communist Review*, October, 679–90.

——— (1953) *Intelligence Testing and the Comprehensive School*. London: Lawrence and Wishart.

——— (1955) *The Common Secondary School*. London: Lawrence and Wishart.

——— (1971) *Intelligence, Psychology and Education: A Marxist Critique*. London: Lawrence and Wishart.

Thom, D. (2004) 'Politics and the people: Brian Simon and the campaign against intelligence tests in British schools'. *History of Education*, 33 (5), 515–29.

White, J. (2006) *Intelligence, Destiny and Education: the Ideological Roots of Intelligence Testing*. London: Routledge.

Wooldridge, A. (1994) *Measuring the Mind: Education and Psychology in England, c. 1860 – c. 1990*. Cambridge: Cambridge University Press.

Young, M. (1958) *The Rise of the Meritocracy, 1870–2033*. Harmondsworth: Penguin.

References for Chapter 6

Burt, C. (1969) 'The mental differences between children', in C. B. Cox and A. E. Dyson (eds), *Black Paper Two: The Crisis in Education*. London: Critical Quarterly Society, pp. 16–25.

Chitty, C. (1987) 'The comprehensive principle under threat', in C. Chitty (ed.), *Redefining the Comprehensive Experience*. Bedford Way Papers 32, Institute of Education, University of London, pp. 6–27.

Denham, A. and Garnett, M. (2001) *Keith Joseph*. Chesham: Acumen Publishing.

DES (Department of Education and Science) (1975) *A Language for Life* (the Bullock Report). London: HMSO.

——— (1977) *Education in Schools: A Consultative Document* (Cmnd 6869) (Green Paper). London: HMSO, July.

——— (1985) *Education for All* (the Swann Report) (Cmnd 9453). London: HMSO, March.

DoE (Department of Employment) (1982) 'New technical education initiative'. *Press Notice*, 12 November.

Gaine, C. and George, R. (1999) *Gender, 'Race' and Class in Schooling: A New Introduction*. London: the Falmer Press.

Grosvenor, I. (1997) *Assimilating Identities: Racism and Educational Policy in Post-1945 Britain*. London: Lawrence and Wishart.

Hearnshaw, L. (1979) *Cyril Burt – Psychologist*. London: Hodder and Stoughton.

Hillgate Group (1986) *Whose Schools? A Radical Manifesto*. London: the Claridge Press, December.

——— (1987) *The Reform of British Education: From Principles to Practice*. London: Claridge Press, September.

Jay, M. (1986) 'The broken contract between schools and their pupils'. *The Listener*, 20 March, 2–4.

Jensen, A. R. (1969) 'How much can we boost IQ and scholastic achievement?'. *Harvard Educational Review*, 39 (1), 1–123.

Joseph, K. (1986) 'Without prejudice: education for an ethnically mixed society'. *Multicultural Teaching*, 4 (3), 6–8.

Kamin, L. J. (1974) *The Science and Politics of IQ*. New York: John Wiley and Sons.

Lawler, J. M. (1978) *IQ, Heritability and Racism: A Marxist Critique of Jensenism*. London: Lawrence and Wishart.

Lowe, R. (1997) *Schooling and Social Change, 1964–1990*. London: Routledge.

Phillips, M. and Phillips, T. (1998) *Windrush: The Irresistible Rise of Multi-Racial Britain.* London: HarperCollins.

Simon, B. (1971) *Intelligence, Psychology and Education: a Marxist Critique.* London: Lawrence and Wishart.

Walford, G. and Jones, S. (1986) 'The Solihull adventure: an attempt to reintroduce selective schooling'. *Journal of Education Policy,* 1 (3), July–September, 239–53.

Wooldridge, A. (1994) *Measuring the Mind: Education and Psychology in England, c. 1860 – c. 1990.* Cambridge: Cambridge University Press.

References for Chapter 7

Benn, C. (1982a) 'The myth of giftedness (part 1)'. *Forum,* 24 (2), Spring, 50–3.

―――― (1982b) 'The myth of giftedness (part 2)'. *Forum,* 24, (3), Summer, 78–84.

Benn, M. and Chitty, C. (eds) (2004) *A Tribute to Caroline Benn: Education and Democracy.* London: Continuum.

Blair, T. (2006) Speech on Social Exclusion, 31 August.

DfEE (Department for Education and Employment) (1997) *Excellence in Schools,* Cmnd 3681. London: HMSO.

DfES (Department for Education and Skills) (2004) *Five Year Strategy for Children and Learners: Putting People at the Heart of Public Services,* Cmnd 6272. London: HMSO.

―――― (2005) *Higher Standards, Better Schools for All: More Choice for Parents and Pupils,* Cmnd 6677. London: HMSO.

Gardner, H. (1983) *Frames of Mind.* London: Heinemann.

Herrnstein, R. J. and Murray, C. (1994) *The Bell Curve: Intelligence and Class Structure in American Life.* New York: Free Press Paperbacks.

Selden, S. (1999) *Inheriting Shame: the Story of Eugenics and Racism in America.* New York: Teachers College Press.

Sullivan, A. (1994) 'Race and IQ: are whites cleverer than blacks?' *The Sunday Times,* 23 October.

White, J. (1998) *Do Howard Gardner's Multiple Intelligences Add Up?* Perspectives on Education Policy No. 3, London: Institute of Education, University of London.

References for Conclusion

Benn, C. (1982a) 'The myth of giftedness (part 1)'. *Forum*, 24 (2), Spring, 50–3.

Brighouse, T. (2004) 'Everyone can walk on water'. *The Times Educational Supplement*, 4 June.

DfES (Department for Education and Skills) (2005) *Higher Standards, Better Schools for All: More Choice for Parents and Pupils*, Cmnd 6677. London: HMSO.

Drummond, M. J. (2004) 'A learning ethic for everybody'. *The Times Educational Supplement*, 25 June.

Gillborn, D. and Youdell, D. (1999) 'Weakest not at the table'. *The Times Educational Supplement*, 26 November.

——— (2000) *Rationing Education: Policy, Practice, Reform and Equity*. Buckingham: Open University Press.

Gould, S. J. (1981) *The Mismeasure of Man*. New York: Norton.

Hart, S., Dixon, A., Drummond, M. J. and McIntyre, D. (2004) *Learning without Limits*. Maidenhead: Open University Press.

Rosenthal, R. and Jacobson, L. (1968) *Pygmalion in the Classroom*. New York: Holt, Rinehart and Winston.

Simon, B. (1953) *Intelligence Testing and the Comprehensive School*. London: Lawrence and Wishart.

Index

160   *Eugenics, Race and Intelligence in Education*